Photo © 1976 Robert Cushman Hayes

Bengal Tiger *Panthera Tigris Tigris*

THIS BOOK BELONGS TO

MICHAEL FRANCIS
XMAS 1982
GRANDPARENTS FOLEY

Some
of my best
friends are
animals

Some of my best friends are animals

Terry Murphy
DIRECTOR OF THE DUBLIN ZOO

PADDINGTON
PRESS LTD
NEW YORK & LONDON

Library of Congress Cataloging in Publication Data
Murphy, Terry.
  Some of my best friends are animals.

  1. Murphy, Terry.   2. Zoologists—Ireland—Biog-
raphy.   I. Title.
QL31.M92A33   596   79-10717
ISBN 0 448 22683 9   (U.S. and Canada only)
ISBN 0 7092 0521 X

Filmset in England by SX Composing Ltd., Rayleigh, Essex
Printed and bound in the United States
Designed by Colin Lewis

In the United States
PADDINGTON PRESS
Distributed by GROSSET & DUNLAP

In the United Kingdom
PADDINGTON PRESS

In Canada
Distributed by
RANDOM HOUSE OF CANADA LTD.

In Southern Africa
Distributed by
ERNEST STANTON (PUBLISHERS) (PTY.) LTD.

In Australia and New Zealand
Distributed by
A.H. & A.W. REED

Contents

The Zoo
In The Park

THERE I WAS WITH a pair of bush babies—those beautiful little creatures with eyes like saucers. The stewardesses were rushing around us, seeing to our every whim and, of course, I was playing second fiddle to the bush babies.

We were coming in low over the Irish Sea to our approach to Dublin Airport—home again. Given half the chance I would have instructed the pilot to make a detour before landing so that I could film the city with my cine camera from the air.

And if this were a film instead of a book, I'd start it right there.

At first all you could see would be mountains—a long low line of them, in every shade of blue imaginable. Then, as you got closer, you would be able to pick out some of them by their shapes—Bray Head soaring majestically into the sky above the town of Bray, and the Sugar Loaf, an extinct volcano. From the Wicklow Mountains your eyes would be led on to the Dublin Mountains which overlook the city. The Two Rock and

7

Three Rock Mountains are easy to spot, each topped with huge piles of jagged granite. Another hill is capped with an outstanding construction—the ruins of the Hell Fire Club, a fearsome and infamous nineteenth-century gambling den, looming up on the very top of a small peak. And away in the distance lies the sleeping Head of Howth with its islands—Ireland's Eye and Lambay—continuing the line of the land into the sea.

Now the full, magnificent crescent sweep of Killiney Bay would be in view, and you might catch a glimpse of the obelisk perched right on the top of the hills by the bay, erected to commemorate Queen Victoria's visit to Ireland in 1900.

The yachts fanning out from Dun Laoghaire harbour would stand out against the shimmering surface of the bay before the plane started to bank in over the flat expanse of Sandymount Strand and head for the mouth of the River Liffey, past two, huge chimneys dominating the mouth of the river, with the vast, grey bulk of the gasometer looming ahead on the left. Strictly speaking, gasometer is a misnomer; it's actually a gas-holder. But from the moment it was built, when I was a small child, it's been known in Dublin as the gasometer.

Gandon's famous Custom House, with its stately, green copper dome, still stands out on the banks of the Liffey but is overshadowed now by the Liberty Hall sky-scraper, appearing strange and alien, towering above the gentle Georgian and Edwardian buildings that it sprang up among.

But nothing will ever altogether destroy the sheer beauty of Dublin city. With the sea at its feet and the mountains rearing up behind it, every street seems to end with a random glimpse of the hills or the sea, and sometimes both.

On up the Liffey now, crossing O'Connell Bridge

which is wider than it's long, a fact that probably gave rise to the legend that O'Connell street, which runs across it, is the widest street in Europe. Then on the other side, to your right, are the Four Courts and opposite is Christchurch Cathedral, perched on a rise, overlooking the city.

Away on your left and covering half a dozen blocks, stands the Guinness brewery where Ireland's favourite drink is fashioned—not, as so many people believe, from the Liffey water, but from water taken from a well in County Kildare.

Coming into view now is Kingsbridge Station, recently renamed Heuston, and just ahead the Phoenix Park, the largest walled public park within a city anywhere in the world. It is a lovely expanse of green, interrupted only by lakes and trees. You might wonder why the tall obelisk there should be erected to Wellington, the victor of Waterloo, but you have to remember that until 1921 Ireland was a part of the United Kingdom and Richard Wellesley, the Duke of Wellington, was Irish born and bred.

Almost opposite the Wellington Memorial is one of the loveliest zoological gardens in the world. It is not very large but it is charmingly landscaped with two dappled lakes and a spectacular backdrop that consists of the entire range of the Dublin and Wicklow Mountains. The largest lake is inhabited by flamingoes and pelicans, and on its edge in a garden of salvia, begonia, flowering shrubs and roses where peacocks stroll, stands a beautiful house. All around it are wild animals – some in enclosures but most of them enjoying a freedom approaching that of a wild-life park.

I have to pinch myself sometimes to make sure that all this is real, that I, Terry Murphy, live in that house with my wife Kay. And that I am, and have been for more years than I care to remember, Director of the Dublin Zoo.

I live as so many people want to live, surrounded by wild animals, and in one of the most attractive houses on one of the most pleasant sites in what I regard as one of the most beautiful cities in Europe.

It's the sort of thing you don't even dare to dream about when you are young. It's the sort of job thousands of people would pay dearly for the privilege of doing. Yet I get paid for living here and looking after the animals which is a joy in itself, because some of my very best friends are animals.

Friends—it's a very human term, implying mutual respect and understanding as well as affection. Of course I cannot truly describe animals as my friends in this way, but it is not absolutely the wrong word. Perhaps by describing one of the closest relationships I have had with a wild animal, I can explain exactly what I mean.

Joey was a chimpanzee who arrived at the zoo as a tiny baby not long after I had first started working there. I watched him grow up, fascinated by every stage of his development. When he was young I spent many hours playing with him in very much the same way that we play with human babies. He had a lot of contact with humans—not just me—and the games we played developed into teaching sessions. Eventually Joey could use a typewriter, a paint brush, a broom—all sorts of things—and he loved nothing better than to show off his abilities. He was openly and warmly affectionate to anyone he knew well, and I must admit that he was certainly my favourite animal.

If we ever wanted to show animals to important visitors or to the press, Joey would perform for us. It was as if he knew exactly what we wanted. He would sweep out his cage or sit down and appear to type a letter while our guests gaped at him with astonishment, and enjoyed watching him just as much as Joey enjoyed the attention and applause.

As he grew older we knew it was necessary to take precautions and to remember at all times that Joey was a wild animal and not the affectionate human playmate he often appeared to be. Adult chimps can be quite dangerous and unpredictable, particularly when they become annoyed or upset. He could, we knew, give a person a nasty bite so we never allowed him to come into direct contact with visitors or guests to the zoo.

However I continued to handle him with confidence. I felt I knew him so well that nothing could go wrong.

One day we wanted to arrange some photographs for the press. I decided to get Joey out of his cage so that we could pose together. I asked the photographer to stand back from Joey's enclosure while I opened it and took out my friendly chimp. I unlocked the door and Joey immediately loped over to me—he knew it was time to perform and was only too pleased to co-operate.

Then, just as I reached into the enclosure to take hold of Joey and lift him out, the photographer decided to take his first shot. He was using a flash and the sudden, blinding light obviously disturbed Joey—he closed his jaw firmly over my hand.

"Now stop that Joey," I said as calmly as I could. "Come along, let go."

He did release my hand immediately but the damage had been done. The bite I had received was really quite severe and blood was pouring from it. I managed to lock the enclosure and then turned to the photographer. He was staring at me in horror, his face completely white and his hands trembling. I thought he was going to faint from shock.

"I'm all right," I said, "but you'd better get me to the hospital quickly."

At the hospital I found the twenty-two stitches I had to have in my hand far more painful than the bite itself. I needed a few days off to recover.

As I pondered the incident I realized that I had become over confident with Joey. I should never have trusted a fully grown wild animal. I expected Joey to behave like a human being and I had not given him the full respect I would give other wild animals. Thinking back over the times I had handled him with ease I saw that until then I had been lucky, in that he had never been upset or agitated in my company. From that time on I took far more care with my animal friends.

But friend he was and never more so than when I returned to see him after that unfortunate incident. As I walked towards his enclosure, my hand heavily bandaged and my arm in a sling, Joey took one look at me, then dropped his head and ambled to the back of his cage. Picking up his blanket he raised his big, soulful brown eyes in my direction and then turned again and crawled beneath the blanket to hide. Joey was ashamed and remained ashamed for some weeks.

His reaction to me was so human. He appeared to appreciate that he had done wrong and had caused me pain. He was not hiding behind his blanket because he was afraid of me or concerned that he would be punished. We had never punished him in any way. No, he was apparently genuinely upset at his own behaviour, and that is a very sophisticated, almost intelligent, reaction to come from a mere ape.

People argue endlessly about the intelligence of apes and whether they act instinctively or think things out for themselves, like people. I cannot honestly say either opinion is correct, but chimps certainly seem to act as a result of *both*: instinct and thinking.

One chimp, which we had living in the house with us for a time, seemed to be utterly fascinated by electricity. Whenever I let him into a room he immediately went for the light switch on the wall. Before switching on the light he would always look not at the switch, which you would think would be the object of interest to the animal, but at the electric light bulb in the ceiling. Then he would flip the switch and observe the effect on light bulb with every sign of satisfaction. That behaviour certainly could not be classed as instinct. But was it a result of conditioning or of cause and effect reasoning?

It is very hard to say which, but some animals do show signs of thinking things out and acting accordingly. Sea otters, for example, break shells to get at the contents by hammering them with stones which they hold in their tiny paws. And chimps in captivity have been trained as Joey was to use basic tools. A chimp I got to know very well showed a little too much dexterity and intelligence on one occasion.

When I first joined the zoo, towards the end of the war in 1943, there were two famous chimps, Charlie and Suzie, who were known up and down the length and breadth of Ireland.

Unlike most other countries, we have only one zoo so it is simply known as "the zoo." At some time or another nearly everybody in Ireland has visited the place. Over the years zoo "stars" have appeared in the Irish newspapers almost as often as pop stars and television personalities; and Charlie and Suzie were always in the news.

At that time the chimps were housed in big cages with two adjoining sections—one within the Monkey

House which provided shelter and one covered only in wire mesh where they could enjoy the open air. The animals could be locked in either section which enabled the keepers to clean their enclosures in peace—and safety.

One morning their keeper, Jack Supple, was doing just that, sweeping the outer area while Charlie and Suzie were safely locked—or so he thought—inside.

Suddenly he heard a rattle behind him and turned around to see Charlie emerging into the daylight only feet away. Somehow the chimp had managed to open the heavy door which divided the two sections of the cage. Jack was out of that enclosure in seconds and unfortunately, in his rush to escape, he dropped his keys—a whole bunch of them fell jangling to the floor. They caught Charlie's eye immediately.

Jack slapped the padlock closed outside the cage and then had to watch, helpless, as Charlie settled down to examine the fascinating tinkling objects his keeper had dropped.

By the time I arrived Charlie had finished seeing if he could eat the keys and was examining them with enormous care—fingering his way through the entire bunch, looking at each one in turn. As we stood watching him, Jack and I were only too well aware that Charlie had seen and heard those keys every day of his life and had watched Jack lock and unlock that enclosure thousands of times. We knew that we had to get those keys back before Charlie remembered the association between the keys and the padlock. Jack asked me to try to distract the chimp while he used the broom handle to flick the keys to the edge of the cage where he could reach them. Charlie glanced at me with disdain as I frantically clapped my hands and called his name. But as soon as the broom handle touched the keys he snatched them up and retreated to the very back of his cage.

Then to our horror he loped across to the padlock and actually started attempting to imitate the operation he had observed Jack carry out so often.

We both tried to grab the keys from him but it was hopeless—he snarled each time our hands came near them and pulled back from the padlock only to return as soon as our hands were back outside the cage.

"He'll never work it out, will he?" I asked Jack.

"Well I'm going to change the lock anyway and fast," he replied. "Better to be safe than sorry."

Jack rushed off—I knew he was feeling guilty about dropping the keys in his haste to get out of that cage but I did not blame him in the least. A fully grown chimp is a big, strong animal, aggressive when roused, and a lot more nimble than a human being. Jack had been absolutely right to run.

I continued to try to grab the keys but Charlie was becoming very agitated and tried to bite me several times.

He had pulled the padlock, which was on a chain, right around to the inside of his cage and I stared in amazement as he managed to place a key in the key hole.

It didn't fit . . . thank goodness.

By now I was becoming frantic, craning my neck in the hope of seeing Jack on his way back.

It was becoming more and more evident that Charlie was quite capable of trying the keys at random until he found the right one and let himself out. We were in a very nasty predicament: a fully grown male chimp on the loose was a prospect I did not want to consider first thing in the morning and to add to my panic, I knew it was almost time for the day's visitors to start arriving.

Using his hands—and remember chimps have prehensile toes so their feet are like hands—Charlie was thoroughly enjoying himself. He had the padlock securely between his feet, leaving his hands free to fiddle with the keys. While I was fascinated by his dexterity and cleverness, I was already working out a plan of action to put into effect if he escaped, and the first part of that plan concerned how I could get away while keeping an eye on him at the same time.

Then Jack came panting up to the cage with several other keepers in hot pursuit. Gently prodding Charlie with sticks and tempting him with bananas, we persuaded him to move back and stay out of Jack's way as he changed the lock.

So far so good, but we still had to get those keys. For Charlie it was great fun—a whole batch of keepers and a bunch of keys to play with.

He would disdainfully deposit the keys on the floor of the cage near the bars to take advantage of a banana or some other delicacy that we had proferred to him. Then, just as we were on the point of scooping the keys out of the cage, he would casually flick them away, just beyond our reach.

We got a longer pole and he left the keys exactly where they were until we were just on the point of retrieving them. Then with another flick of the toes, he whisked them a few inches further away, still tantalizingly out of our reach.

Sometimes he would taunt us openly by pushing the keys right out to the edge of the bars and, just as we were about to snatch them, he would stretch out a languid foot and deposit them neatly and precisely inside his mouth.

This game went on and on.

In the end, we tried another tactic. It was not well planned, or carefully thought out; it was sheer desperation. We all started to shout and roar at him. Suddenly he lost his temper and without thinking what he was doing, took the keys out of his mouth and threw them at us.

Almost immediately he realized what he had done and was furious. For a moment or two he danced up and down in rage, and then, recognizing that the game was over, he retired into a corner of the cage with his back to us in a deep sulk.

What looked like genuine shame when Joey bit me, and Charlie's antics with the keys dropped by Jack Supple, were by no means isolated incidents. At first, when I was new to life in the zoo, as I witnessed such things happening I would think to myself: "Well, that is the most incredible incident I shall ever see in the zoo." But always I would have to swallow my words when, after only a few weeks or even a few days, something else equally astounding would occur. Eventually I came to expect something new and fascinating from each day. Sometimes the animals are infuriating or they manage to embarrass me terribly. At other times they are irresistibly vulnerable and touching—particularly the babies. I shall never tire of watching and learning from them but before I go on to describe some of their antics I must explain how I came to be sharing my life with animals.

Early Days

THE DUBLIN ZOO OR, to give it its correct title, The Royal Zoological Society of Ireland's Zoological Gardens, will be 150 years old in 1980. The gates were first opened to the public in the year after the gardens opened, on September 1, 1831. Although London Zoo preceded it by some years, the public were not admitted to London Zoo for many years so Dublin Zoo can claim to be the first zoological garden to open to the public in these islands and one of the first in the world.

When I was growing up in Dublin in the 1920s, a visit to the zoo was a favourite family outing. And looking back on those childhood visits I can disassociate my present knowledge of every stick and stone in the place and see it again in my mind's eye as I saw it then. It was a very different place in those days; like the city itself it still retained something of a Victorian atmosphere well into the thirties.

From the moment we left our big house in Appian Way, on the south side of the city, it was one great big thrill. We travelled to the zoo by tram. Two trams, actually: one into the centre of the city and another from Nelson's Pillar (now gone like so many famous Dublin landmarks) taking us to the North Circular road entrance of the Phoenix Park.

If we were lucky our tram would be one of the older ones, with an open platform at each end of the upper deck, where you could lean over the wire mesh rails, listening to the swish of the pulley on the overhead wires and watching out for the electrical sparks as the trolley jumped across the junctions. Sometimes it slipped off altogether and the conductor had to manoeuvre it back into place with a rope attached to the end of it. The trams ran on rails called tramlines which were set into the cobblestones of the road. Most of the city streets were then either cobbled or covered in wooden paving-blocks called setts. A lot of the traffic was horse-drawn and the iron shoes of the horses and the iron bands around the wagon wheels would often strike sparks from the cobbles.

The road leading up to the zoo was lined with market stalls, some no more elaborate than prams from which the baby had been temporarily ousted to accommodate a few pieces of fruit. "A penny each the bananas," the old ladies used to chant. They also sold apples and oranges, and cones of newspaper containing a few peanuts. "Nuts for the monkeys. Get your monkey nuts here," they cried.

On through the turnstile in the old thatched entrance house (still there, I'm happy to say, but no longer used as an entrance) and an eager scramble up a slight rise took us to the first of the cages—a monkey house if I remember rightly, with outdoor cages. Various animals would be eagerly stretching their hands through the bars, prepared to investigate and sample absolutely anything that was offered to them at the beginning of the day but becoming a little more pernickety by the evening.

We may have passed peacocks and Chinese geese and other exotic birds on the way but we never noticed them. They did not count. They were not behind bars; they were not dangerous; they were not wild animals.

I remember an amiable elephant that gave rides by the lake and then returned to his quarters, a heavily barred "circus" ring built onto his stable. Here he consumed vast quantities of halved raw potatoes, sold to the public by his keeper, and fed to the elephant who poked his trunk out to receive these offerings.

I remember a couple of large chimpanzees which seemed to spend most of their time trying to demolish their living quarters; a cockatoo that kept calling "Any water? Any water?"; and a vast crocodile that appeared to sleep right through my childhood and youth.

Another big thrill was a giant tortoise on the lawn in front of the reptile house which the head keeper assured us he had known ever since the animal first came to the gardens. When it arrived it was no bigger, he swore, than the palm of your hand. The tortoise was a hundred and twenty years old, he would tell his astonished audience. It never occurred to us that if he had really made the acquaintance of that tortoise when he was a young man that would have made him about one hundred and forty years old. He was not a young man, certainly, but never that old.

There was a sea-lion which did acrobatic stunts in a small, oily pool and baboons with behinds that looked horribly swollen and diseased. When I joined the zoo I learnt that this display was a normal physical condition perhaps designed to attract the opposite sex at mating time and, if so, certain proof that beauty is in the eye of the beholder.

There were a few sad, sinister-looking eagles perched on top of posts in small enclosures with the grisly remains of rabbits around the base of the poles and, near-by, some bears in a pit. They did not appear nearly as dangerous when you looked down on them as the warning notices said they were.

But the greatest thrill of all was the Lion House—once you recovered from the strong acrid smell which blasted you in the face the moment you pushed open the door, making your eyes sting and clinging for hours to your clothes.

The solid, red brick, Victorian building, its interior lined with cages barred with thick iron rods, contained lions and tigers and leopards, all pacing endlessly back and forth. It seemed to me then that they were furious—angered by the frustration of captivity and just waiting for the keeper to make that one, fatal mistake, allowing them to gain their freedom.

Although there was an outer barrier which pre-vented you from approaching the cages too closely, you could still get very close—far closer than you can today. And at feeding time when the growling and snarling animals clawed and tore at the huge chunks of meat you felt very close to the jungle indeed.

Although I remember those early visits to the zoo with nostalgia and affection, I had absolutely no desire at this period of my life to work in the zoo. Indeed I had no particular interest in animals. I went through a stage of keeping hamsters and guinea pigs and pet rabbits, but I soon lost interest and, as the novelty wore off, somebody else had to feed them and clean their cages—usually my father.

I do not think he had very high hopes for me in those days. And I can't say I blame him. For one thing, I was forever playing truant. Sometimes I persuaded my mother that I had a headache or some other imaginary ailment; at other times I set off for school but failed to arrive.

If I had any ambition at all at this period it was to go travelling – anywhere would do but Africa was the place I most wanted to see, a wild continent of rain forests, savanna plains and the bush.

I loved travel books and learned something about far-away places, but very little else. I cannot recall passing a single exam. When, at the sensitive age of fifteen, I was caned for something very trivial, I walked straight out of the classroom and refused to have anything further to do with school.

This upset my father. He was a huge, bearded man and had a great personality; an extraordinarily hard-working and energetic character, coping with three separate careers. He was a civil servant, working nine-to-five each day at the Attorney General's office. After office hours, he ran shorthand and typing classes at home. He had no formal training in these skills but he taught himself enough to open this school and run classes from five-thirty until about nine at night. He soon acquired so many pupils that he had to take on staff to help him. When I left school he made me attend his classes. I resented it bitterly at the time, but I was well taught and it turned out to be extremely useful. In addition to all this he opened a small shop so that he could have an occupation when he eventually retired from the civil service. Before long he had taken on two more shops in the district. He sold sweets and tobacco and called the shops "Terry's"—he hoped that I would eventually take them over and earn my living as a shopkeeper. In those days the shops stayed open until midnight or even later and although he hired people to work in them he would always go round to all three to lock up each night as well as handling the accounts himself.

In between times he smoked continuously and drank almost a bottle of whiskey a day . . . and lived to the age of ninety-four.

When I had completed the shorthand and typing course, he then wanted me to take over the shops. I refused, offering to help out from time to time but no more. I wanted to strike out on my own.

At this period in my life I began drifting; I turned my hand to many things. It's funny, but everything I did came in extremely useful later when I joined the zoo. I worked for a while for an engineering firm and got plenty of practical experience. At the time my greatest ambition was to become an architect. Later, when new enclosures were required for the zoo, I was able to do the working drawings for myself, in order to explain to the architect exactly what I wanted.

For a time I joined a chocolate company, initially doing window-dressing and display, and finally working in public relations. Again, invaluable experience because public relations is an essential feature of running a zoo.

Then the war broke out in 1939. I wanted to fly. To work on board an aircraft in any capacity would do, but my dream was to become a pilot. I was determined to fly and would not even consider the other services.

I travelled to England and tried to get into the Royal Air Force. I was bitterly disappointed when they turned me down on the grounds that I was colour-blind. I know the doctor was right—a colour-blind airman is useless because he cannot identify plane markings or land a plane using the coloured markings and lights on the airfield.

I worked in advertizing and public relations in England for a time—more invaluable experience—and then returned to Dublin and made my one, disastrous expedition into the world of private enterprise. I decided that the way to make a fortune was to discover some commodity that was scarce and to manufacture it. I had a pretty wide choice because almost everything was scarce during the war. I chose toys.

I began by making up some samples—a little trolley with coloured blocks on it and other simple toys for small children. I trotted down to a big Dublin toy shop and bagged a good order. I then discovered that while it was easy enough to make up a few samples, carefully fitting the wooden sections together and laboriously hand-painting them, it was utterly impossible to turn them out in large quantities at an economic price. My absurd mistake was that I had not included either a profit margin or my own time in quoting my prices, with the result that the enterprise very quickly folded.

Then, out of the blue, came a lucky break—and the most decisive moment of my life. A long standing friend of the family's, whom we always called Auntie Manders, asked me one day if I'd be interested in working in the Dublin Zoo.

She was a member of the Royal Zoological Society and on very friendly terms with Cedric Flood, the zoo's superintendant. The zoo was suddenly doing a terrific amount of business because the war had made so many other leisure activities impossible particularly as a result of the petrol shortage. Cedric Flood was grossly over worked and looking for an assistant. If I was interested, she would arrange an appointment.

Cedric Flood had spent most of his life tea-planting in Burma where he had gained valuable experience with many wild animals and especially elephants. His tiny office was out in a service yard—no more than a shed really. We talked about everything under the sun except, curiously enough, animals—the word was not even mentioned. We got on famously but he explained that I could not be hired until the Council had met and approved me.

The Council saw me after one of their regular meetings which take place on one Saturday each month, over breakfast—a Society tradition. The menu invariably consists of porridge, always eaten standing up, followed by a sit-down meal of bacon and eggs with toast and marmalade, and tea. Once a year, in high summer, there is a Strawberry Breakfast when Society members are allowed to invite guests to join them.

Needless to say, I waited nervously outside while all this eating was going on and was then summoned in and questioned by about twelve people. The Council were, and still are, the governing body for the zoo. All major decisions are made by them and this includes the acquisition of new animals and staff.

Like Cedric Flood, they seemed to be supremely unconcerned as to whether I knew anything about animals. They did ask me how I would react in an emergency, if one of the animals escaped for example. I cannot remember what reply I gave but it seems to have satisfied them. It was the fact that I was prepared to work all hours, weekends and public holidays included, that seemed to decide the issue.

In June 1943 I joined the zoo as Cedric Flood's assistant. It sounded very grand, assistant to the superintendant of the Dublin Zoo, but in the beginning it was really a basic, administrative job. I spent hours in that gas-lit shed that Cedric called the office, counting the cash at the end of the day, keeping a note of how much came from the gate, how much from the pony and elephant rides and how much from the shop and tea rooms. I also did the wages book, ran messages, dealt with the mail and helped out wherever I could be useful. There were only two of us on the management side and we handled everything from buying food for the animals to organizing maintenance and repairs to the grounds. The secretarial and membership side was managed by a most delightful lady, Gladys Dunbar (now Randal). She was an integral part of the zoo until she retired in 1959.

From our shed we looked out on to a muddy yard beside some stables. Here was housed the only form of transport available to the zoo—a pony and trap. Every week Topsy, the pony, would be hitched to the trap so that Cedric and I could make our regular visit to the bank and do whatever else was necessary in the centre of Dublin. With the week's takings we'd set off, trotting into town at a steady pace. It was the return journeys that I remember most vividly though. As soon as Topsy knew she was homeward bound she would race along, almost out of control. Cedric and I clung on for our lives as we zoomed through the traffic.

As the months passed, Cedric began to rely on me more and more and delegated an ever-increasing number of tasks. I began to take responsibility for the delivery of animals to the zoo but for many months that was almost the only contact I had with them in the course of my work.

However, after work or during my breaks, I would spend as much time as possible with the animals and it was not long before I began to get involved with them as part of my job. I always jumped at the chance if one of the keepers needed assistance.

I was sitting in the office one morning when a young assistant keeper came in looking worried.

"Where's Mr. Flood?" he said, obviously upset at not finding him there.

"He's away for the day. Can I help?" I asked, immediately assuming my responsibility as second in command but rather deflated by the keeper's reaction.

"Oh well, I don't know about that Mr. Murphy. It's a problem with the elephant, Sarah, you see. Mr. Flood could handle it."

I was on my own and determined to rise to the occasion.

"I'm sure I can help," I said, getting up from my desk, hoping that my positive attitude would increase his confidence.

"Sarah has hurt her foot, I think it's a splinter, and someone has to get it out. Her keeper's off sick, you see. Mr. Flood would normally do it."

I nearly sat down again immediately. We did not have a resident vet at that time and it was clear that if I wanted to get on at the zoo I had to be prepared to handle situations like this. I swallowed hard and followed the keeper out of the office.

The head keeper joined us as we walked towards the elephant enclosure—he was very relaxed and started chatting about the elephants.

"They can be tricky customers, not that Sarah is, but have you ever heard the story about Sita?" he asked.

He proceeded to tell me about an Indian elephant which had been in the zoo at the turn of the last century. Sita proved to be a difficult elephant. She had once thrown her keeper, a very experienced man, to the ground and he'd been hospitalized as a result. However he was not over concerned about the incident and had got along with her very well afterwards.

Then, four years later, when Sita was suffering from an ulcerated foot and the same keeper was trying to treat it, he had obviously caused her pain in some way and she turned on him. My heart sank—but worse was still to come. Sita knocked her keeper to the ground and then crushed his head with her huge foot, killing him.

The head keeper finished his story as we approached

Sarah's enclosure—she was trying to hold one of her back feet off the ground.

"Sita was featured in the *Police Gazette* you know," he added.

I was terrified.

"Now Sarah, on the other hand, has always been a calm and co-operative animal," he said reassuringly.

She certainly looked calm but my eyes went straight to those enormous feet. I took some forceps and a bottle of peroxide from the assistant keeper and approached her gingerly.

She stood perfectly still as I went behind her—it was clearly her left back foot that was worrying her. I put down the peroxide and lifted the foot in my hand. She didn't move a muscle. A piece of glass was embedded in the very bottom of the foot, but enough of it was protruding for me to get a good hold with the forceps and pull it out in one, swift movement.

I was prepared for her to kick me half-way across the zoo but Sarah showed no reaction. I placed the foot back on the ground very gently and poured a little peroxide on a cloth. This was definitely going to hurt her, I thought, even if the extraction of the glass had not.

I glanced up at the keepers—they both smiled and nodded.

Astounded at my own agility, I raised her foot, dabbed it liberally with peroxide, placed it back on the ground, grabbed the forceps and the bottle, and charged out of that enclosure—all in less than thirty seconds.

Sarah did nothing! She was absolutely fine after her ordeal. I needed a large drink.

A few weeks later another task involving handling animals came my way. Again I was very nervous but these creatures turned out to be very friendly. However, you can understand my reaction when I was told to go and groom three cheetah. I immediately conjured up in my mind a picture of three ferocious, snarling cats—hissing and clawing at me as I desperately tried to get near them with a small comb.

They were the first animals we had acquired since the war, apart from those on deposit from other zoos. (Because of the danger of bombing in the United Kingdom and the even greater shortage of food there than in Ireland, we had agreed to look after some big cats from British zoos as well as Bertram Mills' circus tigers.)

The cheetah created a great deal of interest. I cannot truly describe them as wild animals because they were remarkably tame. They had been hand-reared by a dealer and so carefully looked after that they had never learned to groom themselves. My chore was to go into the cage with the three cheetah every day and comb them—just as you would groom a domestic cat in order to remove ragged, tangled fur. They were completely relaxed. I could sit with them in the cage for hours without any feeling of concern and take them out for walks around the grounds.

It was while I was working with these cheetah that I first realized not only how thoroughly I enjoyed handling animals but also that they responded well to me. The more time I spent with them, the more I understood them.

I knew then that the only way to learn about wild animals was not from books or lectures by experts, although they too are important, but from spending time with the animals and watching their fascinating behaviour.

I've been doing just that for over thirty-five years now and I still learn something new about them almost every day.

Marriage
And Monkey
Business

S UCCESSFUL MATING, SO vital to the business of
running a zoo, is also a pretty important element in
the human scheme of things, and I had made my
choice before I joined the zoo.

I'd met Kay in the early years of the war. She came
from Cheshire in England, near the Welsh border. As a
child, it had not occurred to her that she would ever live
in Ireland, much less in a zoo. But her father came over
to Ireland to manage the Irish branch of the company he
worked for. The family separated, Kay's sisters remaining in England with their mother, and Kay coming
to Ireland with her father. His grandmother was
originally from Galway and there was a Spanish grand-
father called Gomez whom Kay liked to imagine was
probably descended from a sailor stranded in Ireland off
one of the wrecks from the Spanish Armada.

Courtship in Ireland in those days proceeded at a
slow pace. We had no choice in the matter, because of the
desperate shortage of money. No young people had cars;
initially, we couldn't afford them, and then the war came

along and there was no petrol. So it was public transport or bicycles. I've always regarded the bicycle as a highly unsociable and extremely hazardous vehicle. Unsociable because if there's any traffic or any sort of a wind blowing, you cannot hear what your companion is saying, and if you move closer together to remedy that defect, there's always the chance that the handlebars will get locked together with calamitous results.

In Dublin City cycling was particularly hazardous. The wooden setts acquired a surface like glass whenever it rained (which in Ireland is a lot of the time) and severe skids were a regular occurrence. Also the tramlines were, for some perverse reason, constructed to dimensions which exactly fitted the depth and width of a standard bicycle tyre. If you were unlucky enough to slide off the greasy cobblestones and get your cycle wheels caught in the groove of a tramline you were stuck there and attempts to extricate yourself usually entailed a disastrous collapse.

Still, a whole generation of young Dubliners met and made their acquaintance on these infernal machines, cycling out to Portmarnock or the Scalp or Enniskerry, and most of them are still together like Kay and myself.

During the latter years of the war and the immediate post-war austerity period, everybody used bicycles even on strictly formal social occasions. There was no alternative. The petrol ration was confined to doctors and other essential members of the human race and there were no taxis. And Dublin being Dublin, not even at the height of "the emergency," as the war years were called in Ireland, did it occur to anybody to drop the white tie and tails and long evening dresses that were always worn on social occasions. It was not uncommon to see a young man in flapping tails and stiff white shirt and tie cycling over the cobblestones with his partner in a long evening dress sitting on the crossbar.

Even before I joined the zoo I remember going to the Zoo Dance. This was one of the big social events of the year in Dublin. Tickets were quite hard to come by and fiendishly expensive by our standards in those days: about thirty shillings (£1.50) each. And drinks had to be paid for on top of that.

The dance itself was held in a huge marquee erected on the lawn. During those war years special facilities were provided for parking bicycles and the Lion House was used as a cloakroom. Other marquees housed bars and restaurants, and most of the animal houses were left open all evening so that guests could wander around between dances and make the acquaintance of the animals. I believe the animals enjoyed the noise and the excitement just as much as the humans did but there were differing opinions on that. Later, when I was director, a lady who remains a very good friend of mine plunged the whole district into darkness by pulling out a plug in the Parrot House because she thought it was unfair to keep the parrots awake all night just for the gratification of a group of socialites. Unfortunately the plug she disconnected was vital to the whole electrical system of the area and there was considerable confusion (not resented by any means by all of the guests, some of whom took immediate advantage of the temporary spell of darkness to get better acquainted). Even with the lights on, the gardens, with acres of bushes and trees and isolated groves of all kinds, were a great place for taking your sweetheart.

Kay and I were married in Cheshire in 1946, three years after I joined the zoo. Initially we lived in an apartment in my father's house in Appian Way.

I worked very long hours—from eight or nine in the morning until eight or nine in the evening, plus Saturdays and Sundays and all public holidays, often with a tiresome wait in a queue for a bus right across town at the end of the day. It soon became clear that we would have to move closer to the gardens. Before long the Council found us a bungalow right outside the zoo walls, in Blackhorse Avenue. Kay was now able to come and join me in the zoo for lunch from time to time but she still did not see all that much of me. I was far too interested in all that was going on in the zoo. I spent hours after work with the animals, especially the chimpanzees—far too many hours for Kay's liking.

Most visitors to the zoo find the apes, and the chimpanzees in particular, the most fascinating of all animals. It's natural enough I suppose, because so many of their characteristics are uncannily "human," and many of their antics highly entertaining.

The main difference between monkeys and apes incidentally—and I'm always being asked this—is that apes do not have tails and they are larger animals than monkeys. There are four apes: the orang-utan, the chimpanzee, the gibbon and the gorilla. And there is one tailless monkey, the Barbary ape of Gibraltar, which is a variety of macaque. Its name is confusing but it is definitely a monkey, not an ape, and the only indigenous European monkey.

Although initially Kay was no more concerned about the animals than I had been, she soon had to take a very active interest in them. Her attitude became very important when we moved into the house in the zoo and had to bring all sorts of animals indoors for special treatment.

We have had young chimps living with us at various times and they were always the best of company. But as soon as they start to grow up, you have to let them go.

With the best will in the world, you cannot keep a fully grown chimp in the house. If he decides to throw himself at you out of affection, he can easily knock you down the stairs. They also become unpredictable and lose their tempers for no apparent reason, and are capable of causing considerable damage around the house.

I'm often asked whether this unpredictable behaviour has anything to do with their being kept in captivity or because they find themselves in an environment that is not natural to them. Obviously it is difficult to keep any large animal in the confined and crowded space of a house but left alone in their enclosures they are usually not at all difficult to look after. Even there, they do act unpredictably at times but it is wrong to try and rationalize their behaviour in human terms. When dealing with wild animals—whether they are in captivity or in their natural environment—people always have to be on guard because even when nothing unusual is happening an animal can suddenly change its behaviour. It's often quite impossible to understand why.

After all, we're not all that good at understanding the motivation of other members of the human race with whom we can communicate in words, at least up to a point, so it really is not surprising that we sometimes find ourselves utterly baffled by the behaviour of creatures from the wild about which we are just beginning to learn.

One of the most extraordinary examples of unpredictable behaviour I have experienced involved one of our gibbons, Bimbo, a character I knew very well indeed.

The gibbons live on an island in one of the lakes, and Bimbo was somewhat notorious for his prodigious leaping ability between the trees.

One day a visitor caught his eye and Bimbo jumped

over more than fifteen feet of water and chased the poor man until he found refuge in the gents' lavatory.

The visitor he chased was an Asian student and it crossed my mind at the time, because Bimbo had never chased anyone or attempted to do so before, that he actually saw this student as a potential enemy because they both came from the same part of the world.

When the student had safely made his escape, Bimbo drifted quietly away, resting on the wall around an enclosure we had built for rhesus monkeys. He settled down quite happily allowing himself to be fed by some children. We caught him in a net, put him in a cage for a day or two to allow him to cool down and then restored him to his place on the island because it didn't seem likely, on the law of averages, that anything similar would ever happen again. I apologized profusely to the student—poor compensation for his experience.

Two weeks later another student from the same part of the world came along and to my absolute astonishment, Bimbo did exactly the same thing: he leapt off the island. We were feeding the sea-lions and there were hundreds of people around, people of all nationalities, but Bimbo picked out this particular person, chased him into a corner and bit the unfortunate man in the neck.

The student was only very slightly injured, although naturally quite shaken. I was horrified and immediately moved the gibbons to another island, a greater distance from the shore.

Gibbons are among the most adroit acrobats in the zoo—in the world come to that. Bimbo had managed to cross the water by swinging from a branch on the island, using his exceptionally long arms for impetus. We made sure that there was no way they could swing to shore from their new home—it was not the first time I had had to move them.

Right from the beginning it was always my policy to put as many animals as possible into an environment where they could have a certain amount of freedom of movement, and where they could be viewed by the public without any obstructions like bars or wire netting. Accordingly, I put the gibbons on an island believing that the intervening water would be barrier enough to keep them in their place. Most apes and monkeys can swim, if they have to, though they don't like the water and avoid it completely if possible. Because of their build, gibbons cannot swim at all.

The first island I chose was far too close to the shore. Within a week, two of them had vaulted on to the mainland and had gone adrift in the Phoenix Park. The first one we found easily enough, up in a tree just outside the zoo fencing. A ring of keepers stood guard around the base of the tree and one of them climbed the tree to get above the gibbon and move him down. The strategy worked extremely well, and once he was down, capturing the gibbon was no problem at all. They are pretty helpless on the ground; they run on their two feet, like humans, and not on all fours like most monkeys and some of the apes. Away from the trees it was very easy to get a net over him, though of course, as usual, somebody got bitten.

The other missing gibbon was Bimbo so I wandered around the park in the immediate vicinity of the zoo calling out his name, hoping that when he heard my voice he would come down out of whatever tree he was hiding in. But we had no luck that day; there was no sign of him.

The next day we heard reports that he'd been seen in a tree in the grounds of the President of Ireland's House which adjoins the zoo and which was always a favourite spot with our animal refugees. There was no further word of him for about three days, but whenever I went out in the car—I had by this stage managed to acquire an old Ford—I chucked a net in the back and a few pieces of fruit with which to tempt him if I happened to come across him.

About four days after his escape I was driving from our bungalow in Blackhorse Lane to the zoo very early in the morning, a quarter-past seven perhaps. It was a clear, sunny, autumn day but bitterly cold. As I drove along the road on the perimeter of the zoo, I suddenly spotted Bimbo. He was just inside the zoo grounds, high up in a tree. I stopped the car, collected a couple of bananas, got out and went to the railings and tried to tempt him down.

I don't know whether it was the sound of my voice or the sight of the bananas, because he must have been hungry after four days, but he came down immediately and I started feeding him through the railings. I did this to re-establish the relationship between us and to regain his confidence. As soon as I had achieved this, I stood back away from the railings and offered him another piece of fruit, this time keeping my hands on my side of the railings. Bimbo, as I expected, extended one long, spidery arm through the railings to reach for the food and instantly I grabbed his wrist. Gibbons are not particularly strong; most of their strength is in the middle jaw and the canines, and of course he could not get those near me through the railings.

He was furious but he realized that there was nothing he could do about it.

His next move was an obvious one, which I had fortunately anticipated. He put his other arm out through the next gap in the railings in order to retrieve the hand I was holding. I immediately grasped his other wrist, and held him firmly against the railings.

Very clever. I'd captured the missing gibbon. And there I was at half-past seven on a bitterly cold autumn morning, holding hands with an ape through the outer railings of the zoo, as powerless to do anything about the situation as he was. There was a net in the car, but there was no way that I could reach it without releasing him. I was absolutely helpless and I felt a complete idiot standing there grasping Bimbo through the bars.

After what seemed like hours, one of the park attendants came along.

"Well good morning Mr. Murphy," he called out calmly, as if he was in the habit of seeing me standing there outside the railings holding hands with an ape every day.

"Good morning be damned," I shouted. "Get one of the keepers at once and tell him to bring along a net."

It could easily have been another hour before anyone arrived. I'd lost all power of judging time and with Bimbo tugging against me I couldn't get a glimpse of my wrist watch. Eventually the monkey keeper crept up with a net, and captured Bimbo from behind before the animal had realized what was happening.

As I let go of his hands he seemed to grin at me, as if admitting that I'd got the better of him this time around.

We moved the gibbons. But it was from the second island that Bimbo managed to chase the two students! The third island was a complete success—until we had a bout of extremely cold weather.

The lake iced over. The gibbons didn't trust the ice at first but then it snowed. The lake suddenly appeared to become an extension of the land because snow had settled all over it. The gibbons began swarming into the rest of the zoo.

Now we move them when the lake freezes but

sometimes we are taken by surprise if it snows and drops below freezing point overnight.

It's always a performance getting them back again, but I think it's a small price to pay for the pleasure it gives to the animals—and the visitors who are able to see the gibbons without bars, in a basically natural situation.

The apes play an important role in attracting visitors to the zoo just by being themselves. Most people seem to enjoy watching their antics and they are wonderful subjects for newspaper photographs. We once had some apes who hit the headlines before they even arrived at the zoo.

We take airplanes for granted these days so it's hard to imagine the excitement that was caused in 1947 by the announcement that Dublin Zoo was about to receive its first consignment of wild animals from America—by air.

A trans-Atlantic service, using flying-boats operating via Gander in Newfoundland and Foynes, near Limerick, before proceeding to the west of England, had been in existence briefly before the war. It had continued, on a skeleton scale, for generals, politicians and VIPs during the war, but it was not until 1945 that Shannon Airport was opened and regular flights by Skymasters and, later, Constellations were introduced. I found it interesting that the site chosen by the Irish government for the new airport was a district formerly known as Rineanna, an old Gaelic word that means the gathering place of birds. Flying the Atlantic at this time was a great novelty and people who made the crossing regarded it as a huge adventure, as indeed it was.

Remembering my public relations days, it had struck me that it would be good publicity both for TWA and for the Dublin Zoo if we could arrange to fly a consignment of animals from New York to Shannon soon after it first opened. The consignment in question consisted of a miscellaneous collection of monkeys and apes, including some chimpanzees which we were bringing in to replace animals lost during the war years.

By this time the zoo had progressed from the pony and trap to a small Ford pick-up truck which had a discreet brass plate on its side revealing, though rather coyly, that the truck was the property of the Royal Zoological Society of Ireland. For this occasion though, I had two big posters printed to announce in large letters: TWA BRINGS IN FIRST AIR CONSIGNMENT OF ANIMALS FOR DUBLIN ZOO. These we pasted on each side of the truck before going down with Jack Supple, who was then the monkey keeper, to collect the cargo.

Everything was brand new at Shannon Airport, and it was all such a novelty that the Dublin newspapers kept a reporter and cameraman in the airport to meet the new arrivals. On average only one plane a day was landing at Shannon so the officials had plenty of time to show us around. We were at the airport for about three days and it was one long, continuous party. We were treated like royalty and given the run of the entire place, including the control tower. When news eventually came through that the plane had taken off from New York, I was invited to have a word with the pilot and see how things were going.

"This is Terry Murphy of the Dublin Zoo. How are the chimps doing?"

"Fine. We fed them some bananas at Gander and they're in the best of form. They seem to like flying. Say, do you think these are the first chimps ever to fly the Atlantic?"

I assured him that to my knowledge they were. I had a couple more chats with the captain *en route* and we were all out on the tarmac when the plane, a Constellation, touched-down. The whole journey from New York, including the touch-down at Gander, had taken fourteen hours, a gruelling flight by today's standards but the animals were all in great shape.

The new arrivals, although they were really no more interesting than any of the other apes and monkeys we had at the zoo, were a big attraction for quite a time, simply because they had crossed the Atlantic by air.

Chimpanzees in their natural environment live in small troops with one dominant male. He can be joined by as many as six adult females and their offspring. The whole group usually consists of no more than twelve or fourteen animals.

This natural grouping can be easily accommodated in a zoo and so as we worked towards showing our animals in more open and attractive enclosures, one of our first projects was to take the chimps out of their separate cages and create one spacious enclosure for an entire troop.

The chimps seemed very content in their new home but one problem did arise.

When they are first born, they cling to the hair of the mother's chest and live exclusively on her milk. As they grow older and bolder, they begin to stray from her, at first only a few feet away, returning regularly to cling on to her hair. In the wild, during these forays, the baby chimps can help themselves to the abundance of food nature provides, and by imitating the older members of their troop they learn how to supplement their milk diet. In this way they gradually wean themselves.

In captivity this natural process comes up against the problem of greed. Unlike mother nature, we cannot provide an inexhaustible stock of tasty food. What we do provide is perfectly adequate for the entire troop.

However the older, more experienced members of the troop, eat it all and providing extra food for the youngsters' mouths does not work. Extra food in the enclosure is soon snatched up and eaten before the babies have a chance to experiment.

In this situation, if a young chimp is to grow healthy and strong, the obvious solution is to remove it from the troop and feed it separately. But this works only if all the chimps are kept in separate enclosures because a troop will not accept an animal that has been taken away from it and reared elsewhere. We were determined, therefore, to keep the young with the troop at all times so that we could maintain a natural group in one large enclosure. To achieve this we had to outwit the adults and help the young get their share of food.

Our task was made easy by the fact that at night we house the chimps in separate compartments. The baby chimps obviously stay with their mother so the opposition was lowered to one adult. In her night quarters we distributed all sorts of tasty morsels—leaves, raisins, bananas. We put the food in every corner we could find, so giving the young chimp a chance of grabbing some of the food before its mother had found it all and eaten it. It worked. The baby chimps thoroughly enjoyed the game of finding the food and so weaned themselves successfully, and gradually they became as adept at grabbring the food in the main enclosure as the rest of the troop.

Gorillas also live in small troops and eventually I hope to establish one at the zoo. But to achieve this the young pair we now have will first have to mate. While we wait for them to reach maturity we do not want to keep them in a small, old-fashioned cage-type enclosure so we have placed them in a very pleasant home with a glass front. The glass is specially laminated, shatterproof and an inch thick—strong enough, one would imagine, to withstand the strength of even a gorilla. But no, they break it continually and we are endlessly trying to find stronger glass.

The orang-utan, unlike most other apes and monkeys, is a nomad. In the wild the male adults often live alone, wandering through the forests, staying mainly in the trees where they swing from branch to branch using their immensely powerful arms. When a male encounters a female in estrous he will mate with her and then continue his solitary wandering.

It is possible to keep them in pairs in the zoo, but rarely in a colony. As with the gorillas, we kept our pair of orang-utans at one time in an enclosure partly built of strong glass and at first there were no problems, but we hadn't accounted for the intelligence of the male, Tommy. And he chose to express it at a rather embarrassing moment for me.

Tommy and his mate, Eve, were youngsters when they first arrived at the zoo. We used glass on their enclosure not only because it gave our visitors an unrestricted view of the animals but, in this case, because glass is also windproof, providing shelter for creatures used to a somewhat warmer climate. The top and front of the enclosure were constructed in wire mesh, and the sides in glass. I was extremely pleased with this highly original design, and particularly because Tommy and Eve, unlike our gorilla friends, made no attempt to break the glass, which was $\frac{3}{8}$ inch thick.

When two visiting zoo directors paid us a call to see how we were incorporating new enclosures with the zoo and to take a general look around, I proudly led them over to the orang-utan enclosure, explaining as we walked along how marvellous it was. The directors were highly impressed and expressed their surprise that the apes had not tried to shatter the glass. Both my visitors had been reluctant to try glass for such powerful and playful animals but now, they admitted, they would certainly use it.

I was still privately wallowing in my success a few minutes later as we returned past the orang-utan enclosure having looked at some other animals.

It was as if Tommy had wanted to take me down a peg or two and teach me a lesson for being so big-headed and self-satisfied. He was sitting smugly on top of his enclosure, looking down on me and my guests with utter disdain. The glass on one side of his lovely, successful, innovative home was shattered! The two zoo directors found this highly amusing and I made a brave effort to laugh it off as I blushed with embarrassment, and glared at Tommy who suddenly managed to look totally innocent and endearing.

Of course there was a simple explanation and it was sheer coincidence that it had happened when I was escorting two guests I particularly wanted to impress. A workman had been repairing the cage next to the orang-utan. He had been hammering and apparently Tommy had watched this with some interest. He eventually decided to try it himself and had "hammered" the glass of his cage until it broke. Great fun!

Tommy is perhaps the most inventive wild creature I have ever had the pleasure to know. He has caused me more problems than I care to remember but his antics, however annoying, are always so ingenious that I cannot help respecting him. Sometimes when I stare into those huge, dark brown eyes of his, set in that almost human face, I wonder what he is thinking, what devilish scheme he is pondering. And I often feel I can detect a wry grin on that face. There is an uncanny sense of communication between Tommy and those of us who know him well, and one thing is undeniable—he keeps us all on our toes.

The night quarters for Tommy and Eve are separated from their outer enclosure by sliding doors. The doors are raised to allow the animals through, and then drop down again. Tommy had watched his keeper raise the partition many times and, sure enough, thought he would try it. He managed to move it by simply pressing his hands flat against the lower half and pushing it up—brilliant! Pushed far enough, he could get his fingers under and keep it open. Tommy soon discovered this and he would encourage Eve to join him on the other side where, of course, they were not wanted.

I had to outwit this orang-utan somehow and I hit upon an idea that I thought was pretty clever. Rather than wedge the door—which is impractical—I suggested to the keeper that we grease it with dripping. The animal fat would not harm Tommy if he ate it but it would stop him getting a grip on the partition. The keeper thought it sounded a fine idea but he was rather sceptical—he knows Tommy even better than I do and, frankly, could not see me outwitting Tommy quite so easily. He was right.

Tommy found he could still raise the partition a little but it slipped before he could raise it fully. This he found decidedly annoying, but a solution occurred to him. He scraped his hands clean on the walls of his night quarters, and, inevitably, eventually removed enough of the grease to allow himself to manoeuvre the partition once more.

The keeper suggested a safety catch to keep the lower half closed. Tommy discovered that rattling the door violently loosened the catch. I think I'll stop that story there before the humans involved look completely stupid! Suffice it to say that we are continuing the battle.

In their extremely attractive indoor enclosure in an elevated position overlooking one of the lakes, the orang-utans are separated from the public by a deep dike which is edged with attractive plants and shrubs.

Tommy's first reaction to his and Eve's new home was predictable—he jumped down into the dike. At first we thought we could easily get him back and that he would get bored with the experience but, of course, he didn't. After several excursions into the dike we decided to take action and we installed an electric fence on the orang's side. We also placed a wire fence along the line of plants to prevent young children falling into the dike. On the visitors' side our precautions worked. Tommy, however, was determined to deal with, and overcome, the electric fence on his side. At first the mild electric shocks he and Eve received when they touched it seemed to work, and there was a strange reaction from Tommy as a result. If I touched the fence on the visitors' side, Tommy, as ever watching my every move, would jump in the air. He was reacting as if *he* had touched *his* fence, and had received an electric shock. He was rather annoyed that I didn't jump at all.

This annoyance developed to aggression and before long he had broken the electric wire by bashing it hard. We humans responded to that by placing springs along the wire. We sat back, satisfied that we had solved, at least, that problem. Tommy had other ideas. His next ingenious move was to wrap the skin of a banana around the electric wire and then pull it. Fortunately the banana skin broke before the wire did but Tommy continued to experiment. Using sweet wrappings from food thrown in by visitors, or even his own fur, he managed to insulate the wire so that he could handle it and break it. It happened so often that we gave up and removed the wire.

Being chased back from the dike was a good game but eventually Tommy got bored and simply stopped doing it.

Our problems were solved. The animals were happy, we were happy, but the visitors made a wrong move. Just a short time ago, on St. Patrick's Day—a public holiday in Ireland—Tommy escaped. It all started when a member of the public foolishly threw one of the bamboo sticks, which hold up the plants, into Tommy and Eve's enclosure. Tommy immediately picked it up and considered how he could utilise this new toy.

His brilliant mind soon found a use for it. In one corner of the enclosure is a shower in which Tommy and Eve loved to romp and splash around. Tommy took the stick and using it as a tool he prized the copper pipe, which carries water to the shower, away from the wall. Gripping this pipe he swung himself over the dike and on to the public passage way. The visitors there were delighted by this display of ingenuity. They didn't realize just how dangerous a fully grown male orang-utan can be.

His keeper desperately moved the public towards one of the exits, while Tommy proceeded to demolish the plants along the dike. Just as the people were hurried out of one door, he walked out of the other door and into the zoo.

The keeper raised the alarm. Thankfully it was a rainy day and the zoo was fairly empty. As we cleared the grounds of visitors, the supervisor Martin Reid got in his car and several other keepers climbed into a van. The emergency drill was in operation. They drove towards Tommy who was wandering down a path by the lake. Stopping a few hundred yards short of him, the two vehicles revved-up their engines in an attempt to persuade Tommy to retreat. It worked. He returned up the path and entered his enclosure through the open doors. Once inside he grabbed hold of the copper piping and swung back across the dike. By the time we got there Tommy was sitting in his enclosure as if nothing had happened!

He raised those big, brown eyes at us. He'd out-witted us all again and that wry grin spread across his features.

above My home in the Dublin Zoo.

overleaf An aerial view of the zoo.

Joey and I enjoy a playful wrestle.

Joey always enjoyed performing—on this occasion he was
displaying his decorating talents.

This cheetah and I had to get to know each other soon after I
joined the zoo—I look rather nervous as I try to gain its confidence.

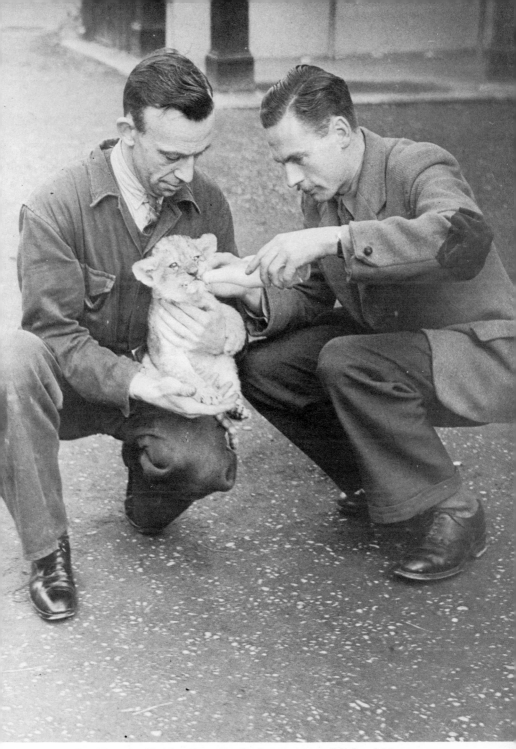

Billy Brophy, the lion keeper, watched over me as I helped him
feed a lion cub.

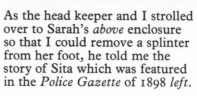

As the head keeper and I strolled over to Sarah's *above* enclosure so that I could remove a splinter from her foot, he told me the story of Sita which was featured in the *Police Gazette* of 1898 *left*.

ROYAL
ZOOLOGICAL GARDENS
PHOENIX PARK, DUBLIN

ORANG-UTAN, CHIMPANZEES, LIONS, TIGERS, CHEETAHS, ELEPHANT, SEA LIONS. NEW REPTILE HOUSE

Open Week-days:—9 a.m. to 6 p.m. in Summer, or to Sunset in Winter. Sundays:—12 noon to 6 p.m.

ADMISSION—Mon. Tues., Thurs. & Fri. - - 1/- Sun., Wed. & Sat. 6d. Children under 13 Half price

TRAMS—No. 5, 9, 22, 23, 24 & 25

Independent Newspapers, Ltd., Dublin.

above A zoo poster from the 1920s.

right The original entrance to the zoo—the thatched cottage is still standing.

Gibbon island—they had to be moved from here after Bimbo
leaped to the shore.

Helping the gardeners.

Chimpanzees—friendly,
inquisitive, genial, talented
and good parents.

Tommy the orang-utan poses with a beauty queen.

Tommy *overleaf* seems to enjoy having his photograph taken but his mate Eve *above* appears rather shy.

Bars, Barriers and Boundaries

THERE ARE A number of misconceptions about zoos in general which I would like to discuss, in particular the widespread misconception about the effect of captivity on wild animals.

Of course there are bad zoos where animals are kept in uncomfortable and insanitary conditions and undoubtedly there are circuses where wild animals are confined. And there is probably good reason for the widespread prejudice against such zoos. Sadly this prejudice acts against zoos of all kinds, even well-run ones. A great deal of this is founded on a fundamental misunderstanding about the nature of animals and a tendency which many people find impossible to resist— to impute human characteristics to animals.

When I first joined the zoo, as well as all our own big cats we had some lions from England and Belfast and some tigers from a circus plus a fine collection of small cats including leopards, pumas and jaguars. The Lion House was full to capacity.

Some people said that the animals looked bored.

These visitors were assuming that because they themselves would feel bored, if confined in a cage with nothing much to do all day, the animals must feel the same way. This is a great mistake: to assume that an animal's requirements and reactions are broadly speaking the same as our own.

In fact if lions appear to look bored that is usually a good sign. In the wild they look bored, it would be more accurate to say content, most of the time—whenever they are not threatened or hunting or asleep. And, from choice, they spend about sixteen hours a day, resting.

If the cats look agitated, I am far more concerned about them. Lions are perhaps the laziest creatures in the world and they take very well to life in a zoo. They have regular food without the necessity to kill or to mark out territory, with no obligation to chase away hyena or jackal or send young pride males packing. Life in the zoo appears to suit them very well.

Also it must be remembered that a great many of the big cats in today's zoos, the vast majority in fact, are second, third or fourth generation zoo animals; neither they nor their immediate forbears have ever known what it is like to live in the wild. Unless they possess an inborn "memory" of the wide open spaces of Africa, which is highly debatable, they have no affinity to the wild. Consequently, there is no reason why they should resent living in an enclosure.

Sometimes people asked the keepers why the lions and tigers, when they were kept in cages, paced up and down, backwards and forwards, vainly trying, it seemed, to get some substitute for the exercise they would get in the wild and venting their pent-up resentment of their cramped home.

Big cats pace up and down, up and down, six or seven paces this way, six or seven that, whenever they

hear the noises which they associate with the imminent
arrival of food or when they are hungry and know it is
time for their keeper to bring food. And they do this re-
gardless of the amount of space that is available to them.
Now that our lions are out in the open, in an enclosure
with a fifty-foot frontage, they still pace up and down
beside the gate where they are fed, covering no more
than ten or twelve feet before turning and retracing their
footsteps.

It is only in comparatively recent years that people
have become wildlife-conscious and have started to
react in this way to caged animals and to object to the
whole principle of keeping animals in captivity.

The Victorians regarded zoos as places where
people could go, and view wild animals in safety. They
cared little about the animals' comfort or even survival;
it took Disney and his brilliant, if sometimes over-
sentimental and anthropomorphizing, wildlife films and
the advent of the excellent television documentaries
about animals in the wild to give people a deep and
genuine interest in natural history and conservation.

In the nineteenth century very little was known
even about the animals' feeding habits. The zoos' principal concern was to keep them alive somehow—for as long
as possible. Even breeding was not a major consideration,
because at that time replacements were easy to obtain
from the wild.

Zoological societies have learned a great deal since
then, and have responded well to the general concern
now felt for the earth's wild animals. But people still
object to seeing animals in captivity, even in modern,
well-designed enclosures, on the grounds that the
animals must suffer from a lack of freedom and are
frustrated.

However, there is no overwhelming evidence that

animals are unhappy in captivity; on the contrary, quite a number of zoo keepers could give evidence that indicates that at least some animals appreciate the security of a cage or enclosure of their own.

There was the interesting case of the three fallow deer.

In a small enclosure, on the far side of the lake, we had three fallow deer. They were not really wild animals; Phoenix Park proper has numerous herds of deer of various species both indigenous and imported, including many fallow deer, so they were not a big attraction.

Dublin Zoo does not cover a wide area. From an original allocation of five acres, the gardens have now been extended to nearly thirty-two acres. As we created new and larger enclosures, changing the style of the zoo considerably, it became obvious that these fallow deer should not be taking up space that could be used for more exotic creatures. We decided that they could easily join the other deer in Phoenix Park where they would have the freedom of a large area of parkland.

They were moved at night. It was a simple operation because their enclosure backed on to the park. The fencing was removed and several keepers escorted the deer to join the herd on the far side of the park. They were left about two miles from their enclosure and they disappeared among the trees.

The keepers returned, the fence was repaired and everyone went home to bed.

Early the next morning, when I was making my rounds, I was staggered to find the three fallow deer wandering disconsolately outside the railings of their paddock, waiting to be let back in. Out of deference to their loyalty, a section of the railings was removed so that they could get back into their old paddock again, where they prospered.

Those three certainly had their choice and did not choose freedom. I kept them in the zoo until I was able to find a good home for them in Donegal, in the north-western corner of Ireland, so far away that they could not possibly have found their way back to the zoo.

Those fallow deer had been in the zoo for years, but it is not necessary for an animal to be in its enclosure for any great length of time before it seems to establish an identity with it and accept that area as its own territory.

As I was doing my rounds one beautiful June morning at about 6:00 A.M., not long ago, I decided to let all the monkeys out into the sunshine.

In the zoo the monkeys are housed in a centrally heated building and each inside cage has its counterpart on the outside with a connecting door in between. During the day the doors are opened and the monkeys are then free to stay either indoors or go out and enjoy the fresh air, as they choose.

This is not normally done until the keeper of the Monkey House arrives but on exceptionally warm and bright mornings I usually open the doors to allow the animals a few hours of extra sunshine.

That morning I went around the Monkey House, lifting all the doors between the inside and outside cages, and most of the monkeys took advantage of my kind offer, including a new animal which had arrived only a few days earlier—a lovely spider monkey from South America, slightly smaller than a gibbon.

I left the Monkey House and proceeded on my usual round of the gardens, having a brief word with the lion pride before letting them out of their dens on to the grass enclosure; saying good morning to the mag-nificent pair of Siberian tigers who greet me either by licking my hand or by jumping into their pool and trying to splash water over me; exchanging greetings with the sea-lion; performing a few antics for the benefit of the chimps who replied in kind; and taking a look to see how a pregnant giraffe was coming along. I was on my way back to the house when suddenly I caught sight of an enormous monkey, sitting on a fence in the middle of the gardens. When I got a little closer I realized that it was our new spider monkey. I couldn't for the life of me imagine how he could have got out of his cage.

This animal and I were almost total strangers but I went over to him, stroked him and said a few words. To my surprise he seemed quite friendly and kindly disposed toward me. I tried to gain his confidence, hoping that I could grab hold of him.

Then suddenly something upset him. He became very nervous and ran off. I thought I'd lost him, assuming that because he was in new and unfamiliar surroundings he would feel disorientated and rush all over the place.

To my amazement, he ran straight back towards his outside cage and right through the front of it. I had to blink before I appreciated what I had seen. Not only had he gone precisely where I wanted him to go but he had apparently passed right through the wire mesh—completely unhindered by it.

I remembered then that repairs to the fronts of all the outer cages on the Monkey House had been in progress the previous day and the men had obviously not got around to putting all the wire mesh back on to the spider monkey's outside enclosure which was open to all four winds.

The interesting point is that the moment he took fright, the spider monkey remembered his home and scuttled straight back there for refuge. When I arrived he was sitting nonchalantly on the floor. He felt safe even though there was nothing between him and the rest of the zoo. I was not sure if he was planning to remain there peaceably so I took up a broom and stood on guard in front of the cage until the first of the keepers reported for duty.

After only two days in the zoo he had come to recognize that cage as his own territory.

This seems to me to make a good case against the notion that all animals hate their cages and would do anything to escape.

Why then do any of them escape, or try to escape? I think there are several answers to that. Apes and monkeys are extremely intelligent and very inquisitive. If you leave a latch or a door or a partition unsecured, of course they'll go through and investigate, out of sheer curiosity. In all probability, left to their own devices, they would return to their cages in the same way as the spider monkey did.

Animals will on occasion manage to escape from their enclosure if upset or agitated, and if one animal escapes, others in the same enclosure often follow suit. Again, they would probably all return of their own accord if we could afford to sit down and wait to allow them to do so. But in a busy zoo we simply cannot do that. Our visitors obviously do not know how to behave when they encounter a wild animal on the loose and most of the animals are as frightened of human beings as the visitors are of them. In that situation an animal could become aggressive. So we have to get them safely back to their enclosure as quickly as possible.

The animals need barriers or bars between themselves and human beings for their own peace of mind as well as for the safety of the visitors.

Bars! That word has ugly connotations; it suggests prison cells. For many years we have been busy removing as many bars and fences as is humanly possible and replacing them with open dikes and glass partitions. Cages and small enclosures are ugly. We have attempted, by using dikes and glass, to give our visitors a clearer view of the animals, and at the same time to provide more space for the animals and, most important, a safer environment for them.

Most of the smaller mammals and birds are now in glass-fronted enclosures. A great many wild animals, the apes and monkeys in particular, are highly susceptible to human germs and viruses. Plate glass not only gives the visitors a clear view and provides a pleasant alternative to those nasty bars but it also lessens the danger, to the animals, of infection.

Nonetheless it did present us with problems—many animals, quite naturally, bumped into the glass and were highly confused by a barrier that they could not see. We whitewashed the glass in some cases or painted mock bars on it. In time, when the animals had thoroughly explored the glass, frequently testing its resilience by bouncing off it, we were able to remove the paint. They had accepted the glass as the boundary of their territory.

We use a glass-fronted cage for Yinka and Gori, our two gorillas. With plenty of poles and perches and chains and ropes to swing about on, there didn't seem to be any reason why Yinka and Gori should not be as pleased with their new surroundings when they first moved in to them as everybody else seemed to be.

But for some reason, they were not. They just sat there sulking. Already I knew both animals well and was used to getting a tremendous welcome from both of them; they would jump about and beat their chests.

But no longer. When I visited them in their new cage, Yinka just stared at me sullenly as if I were a total stranger and an unwelcome one at that, and Gori turned crossly away and sat in a corner with his back to me. It was as if I had offended them.

Their keeper was getting the same reaction.

"I haven't a clue what's wrong with them," he said. "They're eating all right and they seem to be perfectly healthy. They're just listless. But there must be some reason."

We kept a very close watch on them. Not only are gorillas among my favourite animals but they are extremely difficult to replace, so we could not afford to take any chances with them.

Normally, when the public starts to come in, monkeys and apes immediately perk up and go through their antics, because they're great showmen and love attention. But Yinka and Gori just sat there, hardly bothering to glance up at the visitors.

This went on for about a week and gradually they grew more and more listless, to such an extent that I was beginning to get seriously worried about their health, although we could find nothing physically wrong with them.

Then one morning I was in the Monkey House when Gori and Yinka were still confined in their inner sleeping quarters and a keeper was inside their outer cage, cleaning it.

"How do you think they're looking this morning?" I asked him. There was no reaction from him. He continued cleaning out the cage as if I was not there.

Suddenly I realized the problem: he hadn't heard me. The plate glass was completely sound-proof. The gorillas could see us but they couldn't hear any sound whatever from the outside world. They were totally isolated from all the noises they had grown up listening to—monkeys screaming, birds singing—and were locked in a silent world.

Immediately I had an opening cut in the wall of their cage, just above the plate glass, large enough to allow the sounds from the rest of the zoo to reach them.

They perked up at once and inside a day were back to their old form again. Two-way communication had been restored.

Whenever we create a new environment for the animals, we know that in spite of all our careful planning and consideration, the animals themselves will have to let us know if it works.

When we first decided to put our lions outdoors, we used a kind of grotto enclosure with a mountain of rocks at the back and a platform at the foot of this. Between the platform and the public path was a dike filled with water.

The idea was that there should be no visual obstruction at all between the visitors and the lions. The animals would regard that dike as the limit of their territory and the public would have an uninterrupted view of them. Under the mountain were heated dens where the lions could eat, sleep, breed and, we hoped, bring up their young.

It didn't work. We transferred a pride of lions to this attractive grotto and they emerged on to the platform, apparently in open countryside with nothing between them and the public. They immediately retired to the dens underground from which they refused to emerge, no matter how we tried to lure them out. The lack of an obvious boundary was making them nervous. They could not recognize the limits of their territory and clearly felt far too exposed to human beings.

We built a row of rudimentary bars along the edge of the dike hoping that would help and it worked fine. The lions could see that there was some kind of barrier there, so they felt secure enough to come out of their dens and take advantage of their spacious, new, well-demarcated territory. Later, when they became thoroughly accustomed to their new surroundings, we were able to take the bars away.

In the limited space which we have I like to think that the Dublin Zoo creates the most pleasant and spacious environment for our animals that it is possible for us to provide.

Ideally, of course, I'd like to see a large section of the Phoenix Park turned into an extension of the zoo. We could then display animals like impala, which I cannot keep at the moment because you need to see a whole herd with plenty of space for them to move about in before you can appreciate their grace and agility.

We do keep a few species of small antelope in the zoo and there are plenty of deer in the Phoenix Park.

We have a pair of wildebeest (more commonly known as gnu) from which we have bred successfully. We have also bred many blackbuck—a most attractive antelope once widespread throughout India and other parts of Asia but now increasingly rare in their natural habitat. These are extremely lively little animals and although quite small—they're only about four feet long and a little over two feet high—they can easily clear a seven-foot fence, leaping a distance of up to twenty feet in one jump if disturbed.

A single calf may be born at any time of the year, and when the female has dropped her calf she will hide it in a tall tuft of grass where it will remain without moving, even when she wanders off, for at least two or three days until it is steady enough on its feet to follow her around and fend for itself. If any other animal approaches the tuft of grass where the calf is hidden, the female will run off in a different direction to create a diversion and distract the intruder. The females are without horns but the male has magnificent horns up to two and a half feet long with two and sometimes three spiral twists.

The only other antelope we keep are duiker—a very small and graceful African species with huge, moist eyes —and again we bred from them without encountering many problems though we did create zoological history with a female duiker which had five caesarian operations, all successful. They were performed in the Veterinary College in Dublin. The calves were all perfectly healthy and the births didn't seem to do the mother the slightest bit of damage; she lived out her normal lifespan in the zoo.

We simply do not have the space to keep the larger and heavier species of antelope and even if we did have the space such animals are not really suitable for the Dublin Zoo. The ground gets very soft in the winter and such heavy animals would soon churn it up into soft mud which would ruin the grass we have in the zoo; and you can't keep antelope on a hard surface like concrete. However, if we had a large park at our disposal then animals such as this could be kept.

But a wildlife park could house many other creatures as well as antelope. Elephants, zebra, giraffes, polar bears and many more could be kept on spacious open ground, separated from the public and one another in the same way as they are in the zoo—using dikes and moats. But my plans for a wildlife park are still very much just that —plans. Meanwhile the zoo is still changing, new enclosures are being built and, perhaps most significant, the creatures we now keep are beginning to reflect more and more the international concern for protecting and breeding species that are becoming extinct.

Today there is great concern for the conservation of wild

animals, but perhaps as a result of this, many people regard zoos as a threat to wildlife in its natural state. Their argument is simple: for every animal in captivity there is one less animal in the wild. Zoos are seen as yet another example of human beings selfishly depleting the earth of its wild creatures, and in this case just so that they can go and look at the animals at their leisure.

I absolutely agree that people are, and always have been, the greatest single enemy of wildlife. This is not because we kill animals for their flesh or hide, or snare them for zoos and circuses, although we certainly do all of these things. In fact the number of animals shot by the big game hunters, killed for food or captured for zoos, circuses and safari parks, would not make any great difference to the sum total of the wildlife in the world if the environment in which the wild animals live remained unchanged. Most animals would naturally breed again very rapidly, given adequate space and suitable surroundings.

Where we humans have dealt a real death blow to many wild species is not by hunting them down but by taking over their habitat and cultivating it, building fences, roads, railways, cities, airports, dams, mines and industrial sites all over it. That is why there are so many endangered species today; they cannot compete with man for the only kind of terrain on which they can survive.

A point often missed by the opponents of zoos is that by taking endangered animals and breeding from them, it is possible not only to keep rare species alive in captivity but in some cases to restock areas of the wild. Animals of all kinds bred in zoos have been restored to the wild. In this way zoos are beginning to play an important role in the conservation of animals in the wild.

To give just one example, the Arizona Zoo in the

United States has collected, with the help of the Fauna Preservation Society, as many Arabian Oryx as possible. These creatures are now virtually extinct. The zoo has been successful in forming a breeding group and Arabian Oryx are now being returned and set free in areas of the Middle East where it is hoped they will breed and once again become established in their natural environment.

In its heyday as a lion breeding centre—the period between the turn of the century and World War II—the Dublin Zoo was sending cubs all over the world: to Australia, India, Ceylon, Canada, Trinidad and many other countries, including Africa, the original home of lion. In fact, some of the wild lions so eagerly photographed by today's visitors to the safari parks in Africa could be descendants from lions born and bred in the Dublin Zoo.

Some Bright Birds

IN 1952, when I had been at the zoo for almost ten years, I unexpectedly found myself in charge because of the sad and sudden death of Cedric Flood. For a short while I was acting superintendant.

I had no intention of applying for Cedric's job—I knew I was too young and inexperienced to be considered. My father had something to say about that. He insisted I at least fill out a formal application which I eventually did. I had been absolutely right—I didn't get the job. But my father had also been right—the Council now knew I wanted to run the zoo and I became an obvious candidate for the next occasion when the post had to be filled. But that was not for almost five years.

Cedric's successor was Cecil Webb. He had great experience of hunting and collecting wild animals and came to us from the London Zoo where he was Curator of Mammals. In spite of this, his main interest was birds. He could not have come to a better spot than Dublin Zoo.

The first thing he asked me on arrival was why we

did not have the phoenix as the symbol of the zoo since we were located in the middle of the lovely Phoenix Park.

He had assumed that there was an historic association between the park and the phoenix, the legendary bird that set fire to itself every five hundred years or so and then arose, rejuvenated, from its own ashes. There is a statue of a phoenix in the park, donated by a well-meaning but in fact misinformed benefactor. The park is named after that wondrous bird for no other reason than a slip of the tongue.

The park originally derived its name from a famous spa well, a source of clear spring water with alleged health-giving properties. The Gaelic words *fionn uisge*, pronounced, very roughly, "fune ishgeh" and meaning clear water, were mispronounced by non-Gaelic speakers and *fionn uisge* very soon became Phoenix.

The spa well was situated on the perimeter of what is now the Zoological Gardens and the block of houses in which some of the park keepers live is still known as Spa Lodge. The spring itself became contaminated when a Dublin drainage system was being constructed and for many, many years no one was sure where the original spring was located. During excavation work prior to the building of the present Hippo House in 1958, several sections of very ancient, wooden water pipes leading from Spa Lodge were unearthed and are now in the Board of Works Museum. Someone suggested we invite a water diviner to find the most likely site of the original spring as it was obviously in that area. The diviner found the exact spot and a plaque has now been placed there— next to the sea-lion enclosure.

The phoenix, then, had no association with the zoo but we did have plenty of real, live, exotic birds to capture Cecil Webb's keen interest.

One chilly October morning, soon after he arrived,

Cecil approached me looking rather puzzled. He explained that he had just wandered down to the lakes to see one of our most beautiful exhibits—the Indian bar-headed geese. About thirty-five of them lived there and we'd had these delightful geese in the zoo since the 1940s.

That day they were gone—vanished.

"Oh, it's a cold day, very quiet in the zoo—they'll have popped down to St. Stephen's Green," I told Cecil. He looked bemused.

"They'll be back," I said, "probably on Sunday morning. They usually come back in time for lunch on a Sunday."

Cecil was mystified. "How on earth do they know if it's Sunday?" he asked. "And anyway, why do they go into the city in the first place?" He obviously thought I was pulling his leg, so I told him the whole story.

Those geese are very intelligent birds. They know very well that when the weather starts to get cold, hardly anybody comes near the zoo during the week, so they move out to the handiest pond in the city centre where there are plenty of people around to feed them. I had seen them there; all the office workers from around the green were sharing their sandwiches with them. But on Sunday they return to the zoo in the afternoon. They still do it today—they come circling in, regular as clock-work, and settle down on the lake as if they have never been away.

How do they know it is Sunday? I had puzzled over that one for ages when I first noticed this behaviour. I still don't know for certain. It could be the sound of church bells ringing; Dublin is a great city for church bells on a Sunday morning. Or it could be the lack of traffic noise. St. Stephen's Green, normally one of the busiest sections of the city, is still and deserted on

Sunday morning so there is no one around to feed them. Throughout the winter, they are away in the city all through the week, picking up whatever is going in the way of free food, but on the quiet Sunday mornings they know they can find at least a few visitors, and some food, at the zoo—so back they come.

How they ever discovered the existence of St. Stephen's Green is another mystery. Presumably they took off from the zoo lake, made a few tentative reconnaissance flights, widening the circle all the time, until they spotted a couple of places where there appeared to be patches of water big enough for them to land in safety. Having established that this was indeed possible on the ponds in St. Stephen's Green, where there was an adequate runway with no serious obstacles on the approach path, I suppose they began to explore the amenities of the place as an alternative to the zoo from the viewpoint of extra rations.

Every spring, as soon as the weather grows milder, the geese return to the zoo permanently and start to nest on the islands in the lake.

That is with the exception of one pair whom we call George and Liza. These two appear to dislike the community existence on the zoo island which the geese share with swans and ducks. They always find somewhere in Phoenix Park to breed; I think myself that they make their nest in the President of Ireland's property. Probably they feel it gives them a social edge on the others.

For many years when they had hatched out their clutch of goslings, they returned to the zoo, with their brood, on foot. The performance was always the same: they would lead their babies to the zoo boundary and then fly over the top of the railings themselves. Their goslings would run through the gaps between the bars to rejoin their parents inside the zoo, where they would form a neat line and proceed in a leisurely fashion down to the lake. How they managed to find their way back on foot to the zoo from whatever point in the park they had hatched their young always eluded me. It would be simple enough from the air, but goslings cannot fly.

Then one year, not long ago, we had to put wire netting along the boundary railings that run right around the zoo because we'd been losing a lot of valuable animals and birds as a result of raids by foxes and otters.

When erecting the wire we knew that it was going to pose a problem for the geese. The goslings would be unable to get through the netting, and they would be too small to fly over the top. All we could do was watch out for the imminent arrival of George and Liza and their brood and do whatever we could to help out.

It was several months later, on the Whit Monday public holiday, with the zoo crowded and everyone very busy, when George and Liza emerged proudly from the park, their goslings wobbling along in tow.

There seemed to be something happening on the road near the main entrance—horns were blaring and voices were being raised. I went across to see what all the commotion was about, and at first I thought someone's car had broken down and was blocking the traffic. As I got closer I spotted one of the keepers.

"It's George and Liza," he called to me, "and they're trying to cross the road."

Once there was somebody on the scene to explain what was happening everyone was highly co-operative.

George and Liza were several hundred yards from the nearest break in the zoo boundary—the main entrance—and on the wrong side of the road. Stopping the traffic completely, we cleared a path for them to cross the road. We then had to confuse the poor geese by blocking their normal route into the zoo via the railings. George eventually broke through and flew across. Liza followed. We stood back, hoping that these intelligent creatures would soon realize why we wanted them to take a different route.

The goslings were stranded outside the zoo, chirping as loudly as they could and desperately trying to force their way through the wire mesh. The adult birds quickly studied the mesh themselves, then flew back over the railings.

We cleared a path along the road to the entrance and asked the people queuing there to stand aside. By now the traffic had been stopped for quite a distance and a crowd had formed.

George and Liza and family set off in procession down the road and then marched through the turnstiles into the zoo. Loud applause erupted as they headed down to the lake.

The whole performance has been repeated many times since and, incredibly, it always seems to occur on that same public holiday each year. But now the human beings involved are as well trained as the geese, who follow the same turnstile route, and the whole ritual passes off with almost military precision.

The wire mesh was successful in dealing with the enemy from without; unfortunately we had not reckoned on an enemy from within. A raccoon escaped from his enclosure, swam across the lake—they are very good swimmers—and robbed the island nests of all the bar-headed geese eggs. After that they all flew away, except, of course, for George and Liza.

The flock returned in the summer and followed the regular pattern during the winter of stopping by every Sunday. But in the spring they disappeared, to breed elsewhere.

That was not, however, the end of the story. I was in my office one morning when one of the Howth fishermen telephoned me to say that he had seen a large number of very strange-looking birds nesting on Ireland's Eye, a small rocky island near Howth Head on the northern side of Dublin Bay. From his description it sounded as if these might well be the missing bar-headed geese.

As soon as I put the telephone down, I called Martin Reid, the zoo's supervisor, on the intercom. "Feel like a boat trip out to Ireland's Eye?" I asked.

I think he thought I had gone out of my mind, but I explained to him what the fishermen had said and added that if these were indeed our bar-headed geese and if they were indeed breeding out on Ireland's Eye, we could at least climb up and try and collect some of their eggs in order to hatch them in an incubator. This was not cruel; they stood little chance of survival against the seagulls on the island. Gulls are predators and would probably eat the eggs, or the young birds as soon as they wandered from their parents.

Also, these geese are rare and beautiful, and I very much wanted to see them breeding on our lake once again.

That afternoon saw Martin and me clad in oilskins and huddled up in an open motor-boat headed for Ireland's Eye. It's not a very tough climb by mountaineering standards to where the geese had been spotted, but it is sheer rock and pretty steep; quite an ordeal for a pair of zookeepers not in peak condition. However, we eventually made it and found the nests, which the geese had deserted on our approach. We gathered a number of eggs and brought them safely to the zoo. They hatched very successfully and in that way we replaced our resident stock of bar-headed geese.

As soon as they were fully grown, we pinioned them so that they would stay and breed. One wing is disabled, without causing pain to the bird, so that the geese cannot fly away. Their offspring are not pinioned because they return instinctively to join the birds in their parent's colony. This same procedure is adopted by all the major bird sanctuaries to ensure that rare birds nest and rear their young in safety.

Keeping exotic birds on the islands in the zoo lakes has one distinct disadvantage. Capuchins and gibbons are also kept on islands in the lakes. The Capuchin monkeys, which come from South America, are attractive little animals with wistful faces and dark eyes. They get their name from the peak of black hair on the top of their heads—it looks exactly like the cowl of a Capuchin friar. They are the original organ grinder's monkey.

It was originally believed that capuchins were strict vegetarians. Unfortunately that is not so and they are particularly partial to a portion of wild duck now and then. Ours occasionally get the opportunity to capture a young duckling that is unwise enough to stray on to their island. The monkeys work as a team, and head it off very skilfully. Most of the ducks keep well away from the island but when it happens it's inevitably the rare and expensive species that the Capuchins bring down.

Today they can cost roughly £100 a bird; that's the kind of diet the Capuchins are getting.

They wouldn't have to pay anything like that even in an expensive restaurant in Paris.

Seagulls are also extremely bright birds and they cause me endless problems. But there are few sights more beautiful and moving than a seagull slowly circling in a gentle up-draft of wind.

Dublin is famous for its gulls. Seek the first impression of anyone who has just visited the city for the first time; it's a safe bet that they will include the screaming of the seagulls. That's the sound that always wakens you, even in the heart of the city.

In the zoo, they are a menace. We feed our penguins, seals and sea-lions on fresh fish, and whatever time we decide to do it, word always gets around among the seagull community. They are quite capable of catching the fish between the time it leaves the keeper's hand and reaches the penguin's beak. It's incredible how they can fly. I would have to admire them if they were not such a nuisance.

Every day at feeding time, four o'clock on the dot, they arrive—legions of them. How do they know what time it is? In the same way, presumably, as the bar-headed geese know that it is Sunday. They perch row upon row on the animal houses, making a terrible mess. And when the fish appear, they seem to get very nearly as much of it as the birds and animals for whom it is intended.

We have tried to trick them by varying the feeding times, but that only made matters worse. Realizing what we were up to, they took to arriving early in the morning and hanging around all day, just to make sure that they did not miss the free food.

We tried a scare gun. It terrified the visitors, even though we had warned them on the public address system; but it didn't affect the seagulls one bit.

It is not only the fish destined for the sea-lions and the penguins that they steal. They are also particularly adept at seizing very young ducklings. Wild mallards join our exotic birds on the lakes and they often hatch up to twelve or thirteen young. We are completely unable to protect the offspring of these common ducks.

However, the mallards produce such large numbers of eggs that many of them survive despite the seagulls.

When our more precious birds start to breed, we leave the eggs with the mother for as long as possible because she can do the job of hatching them out far more efficiently than any incubator. But we have to watch them very carefully because the principal danger at this stage, now that we have the foxes under control, is another species of predator: small boys whose hobby is bird-nesting. The birds that nest on the islands are safe enough from this menace, but those which nest in the reeds along the edge of the lake are always in danger of having their eggs stolen; and there is nothing much we can do about this because it would take a whole army of keepers to monitor the behaviour of all the small boys that come to the zoo on a busy spring day.

As the baby birds are very vulnerable to predators of all kinds during the first few weeks of their life, we normally take the eggs from the nest when they are just about ready to hatch out, and transfer them to the incubator, not returning the birds to the lake until they are old enough to fend for themselves.

In the case of the less valuable birds we allow the mother to complete the hatching process herself and one of the most fascinating sights in the world is to watch a young duckling which has just emerged from its shell. In the final few days before it hatches out, the mother is actually talking to the baby through the shell, so that when it emerges it already knows the sound of her voice. I've watched a nest where a young duckling has just emerged; instead of going to the mother, it often remains where it is, quite motionless, probably because she has sensed some danger and has given the alarm call which the baby recognizes instantly. A little later, when several other ducklings have emerged from their shells and the danger, whatever it was, has passed, they will scatter in all directions. The moment she calls them back, they'll go straight to her, even if there are half a dozen other ducks nearby. It's quite extraordinary, but they never go to the wrong duck.

Breeding tropical birds is a real challenge because most insist on making their own nests, so we have to provide them with the right environment in which to site them and the right materials from which to manufacture them. This requires endless experimentation and study before we get the materials exactly right.

For example, we've been keeping flamingoes on one of the lakes for about twenty years, and only this year did we succeed in breeding our first flamingo.

We collected mud from every part of the zoo hoping at least one sort of mud would be of the correct consistency for the nests. We placed a tap by the lake so that we could keep the mud moist at all times. I then built several nests based upon descriptions and photographs of flamingo nests in the wild. I'm not sure whether it was the right mud or the new diet we provided but for the very first time since they had been in the zoo the flamingoes actually displayed to one another—performing a ritualistic dance as they do in the wild before mating. I was thrilled and as we watched over the weeks we noticed that one pair was beginning to build a nest of their own. The others followed suit and we soon had ten nests alongside the ones I had built. Mine were completely ignored!

Each pair produced one egg and as the incubation period started we began to get rather nervous. The ten nests were very close together and endless squabbles erupted between the various birds. I spent long hours watching them but I knew I should not interfere. Both the males and females incubated the eggs and eventually one of the eggs hatched. An absolutely delightful, fluffy little creature emerged.

Both the parents fed it with a milky substance that is produced up into the beak from inside the flamingoes. None of the other eggs showed any sign of hatching but the flamingoes continued to sit on their nests.

One morning we experienced a near catastrophe with our one baby flamingo. It fell out of its nest and waddled too close to other birds. We watched in horror as they pecked at the baby. A major fight broke out when the parents went to their baby's rescue and at that point I decided to intervene. I went in among them, picked up the baby as the adult flamingoes fled and placed it back on the nest. The tiny flamingo was so scared and confused it simply would not stay on the nest. I realized I was doing far more harm than good so I stepped well back. Slowly the adult flamingoes returned to their nests and the mother tried to help her baby back but it didn't quite make it. Eventually, after several attempts, the tiny flamingo climbed up to join its mother and slipped under her wing. Its little head peeped out and I breathed a huge sigh of relief.

It became clear that several of the eggs were infertile and that others, if they hatched at all, would hatch too late in the year for the baby birds to survive the cold weather. I removed them all but our one little success has grown up strong and healthy, and we confidently expect more of the adults to breed healthy youngsters next year.

We've helped many other species to breed. The Cape penguins, which come from South Africa, normally live in burrows which they fill with leaves and stones. As the leaves start to rot and ferment they provide heat and humidity which combined with the heat produced by the penguins themselves creates an ideal environment for hatching out the eggs. I tried placing a few beer barrels on their sides, with a small opening cut in one end, to let the birds in and out. We found that as soon as they became used to the barrels, they started to fill them up with leaves and stones, and used them as they would use the burrows on the Cape coast. The Cape penguin normally lays two eggs and we found that they had no problems at all hatching their young in these old barrels.

The King penguin, from Antarctica, lives on the ice floes. Both male and female share the chore of hatching the single egg, which they hold on their feet. They have a fold of skin and feathers which drops down over the egg as they walk and this keeps it warm. When they want to feed they have a way of transferring the egg from one bird to the other without letting it touch the ice or snow. We had a lot of trouble trying to breed King penguins because they do occasionally drop the egg, and while this does no harm on the soft snow that covers the ice floes in their natural habitat, in the zoo, their enclosure had a concrete floor and the eggs often broke. To prevent this we covered an area with soft sand at breeding time.

The sun bittern is a beautiful bird from Central America with a long pointed beak and in the breeding season they make their nests with mud. They are extremely fussy about the exact consistency of the mud that they use. I had a pair of bitterns in a large enclosure with a number of other species of birds. We knew they were a male and female and that in the ordinary way they would move around and collect samples of mud of various consistencies and mix them together until they got it right. In the enclosure there wasn't anything like a sufficient variety of mud for them to do this, so we collected samples of clay from all over the gardens. I put this into the enclosure on a home-made wire nest and to my delight, they accepted it. After working on it for some time they made a nest that was to their liking and reared a number of young in it.

The birds which wander loose around the grounds make their own arrangements for coping with their young. Our peacocks, for example, are given free range of the gardens and we don't have to worry about them. At night they go up into the trees where they are quite safe from foxes and other marauders. When they are ready to nest, they find some spot that is very well concealed, inside a hayshed perhaps or under a bush, and make their own nests there from materials they pick up around the grounds. It's remarkable how well they hide their nests; in all the years I've spent in the zoo, although we have quite a large number of pairs in the gardens, I've only very rarely come across a peacock's nest. Usually the first indication that the peacocks are breeding is the sudden emergence from under a bush of a peahen followed by four or five youngsters—which are very active almost from the moment of birth. In a matter of hours they are wandering away from the mother and searching for little bits of food.

We have never been successful in breeding ostriches in the Dublin Zoo. They have laid eggs but so far all of them have been infertile. We have been able to rear quite a number of rheas, a type of ostrich which comes from Patagonia and the mountains of western South America, as well as several emu, yet another type of ostrich from the dry open plains of Australia.

The principal enemy of the ostrich breeding in the wild is, curiously enough, another bird; the Egyptian vulture. This is an unusual bird in that, like certain species of monkey and ape, it has learned to use what might be described as a rudimentary form of tool. Just as some apes and monkeys will use stones to throw at a leopard, or sometimes even employ a stick to defend themselves, the Egyptian vulture will pick up a heavy stone and drop it with deadly accuracy, like a dive bomber, on to an ostrich egg. It's the only way it can break the shell of the egg, which is over one-sixteenth of an inch thick, and it's well worth breaking because ostrich eggs weigh about three and a half pounds apiece, so there's plenty of nourishment inside.

Our ostriches do not have to cope with Egyptian vultures but, as with so many exotic birds, the major problem in breeding is finding precisely the correct environment, diet and nesting materials. We have not yet discovered why our ostrich eggs are infertile but I hope that eventually we will have success in breeding them.

If there is one species that is an exception to the rule that birds are intelligent creatures it is the ostrich— they are extremely dim. I've known one to settle down close to the railings on a frosty night and in the morning it was discovered frozen to death. Another managed to strangle itself by shoving its neck out through one gap in the railings and then in through another, getting itself hopelessly stuck between two bars.

They are also extremely stubborn. If you want to move one you can only do it by putting a hood over its head. If they can't see where they are going, they become completely docile and you can lead them anywhere. This may well be the origin of the head in the sand legend.

Their whole strength is in their legs. Ostriches do not fly though they use their rudimentary wings to lighten the load that gravity imposes on them and this enables them to run at a tremendous speed.

I was sitting at my desk one morning when I happened to glance up and see, out of the corner of my eye, an ostrich streaking down a hill through the visitors. He must have been doing at least twenty miles an hour. I rushed out and we eventually found he had fallen exhausted near a bush by the gates. There's only one safe way to recapture an escaped ostrich and that's to sit on it, before it can get back on its feet. Usually a couple of us would have thrown ourselves on top of the bird and kept him down, until another keeper came along with a box. But this one was so worn out that we merely had to watch him.

Ostriches are funny in so many ways—the way they look, the way they move, the way they behave—but the most ridiculous thing about them is the things they eat. Sadly, they often kill themselves by swallowing something harmful. They are especially attracted to bright, metallic objects.

A post-mortem was carried out on an ostrich which died in the zoo and we found it had taken in a steady diet of sticks, coins, and the odd key. But even stranger, we found a rather battered prayer book that had also passed down its long, spindly neck—dropped by a Sunday visitor no doubt, who should, perhaps, have been elsewhere.

Animals
On The Loose

CECIL WEBB RESIGNED in 1957 to take a post in
Africa. I felt that I was still a little young in the
eyes of the Council to be made director (the term
superintendant had been dropped), but at least I now
had plenty of hard, practical experience, and I applied
for the job with rather more confidence than I had in
1952. And I got it.

Kay and I moved from the bungalow in Blackhorse
Avenue into the house in the zoo. My father moved in
with us shortly afterwards. He was eighty at the time
and had been very ill. We thought he would be with us
only a matter of months at the most. As it turned out, he
lived with us there for fourteen years. I don't think that
he ever developed any keen interest in the animals but he
loved wandering around the grounds, chatting to the
visitors and the keepers. I encouraged him in this but
made one firm rule: he was never to repeat to me anything he had heard from the keepers. I did not want
them to feel that they could not speak openly.

When, at the age of ninety-four, he contracted

pneumonia and was being taken down to the ambulance on a stretcher, he said to me: "Terry, look in that wardrobe over there and you'll find a bottle of whiskey. Get it for me. It's the only kind of medicine worth a damn." I went to the wardrobe and took out a bottle that was about three-quarters full.

"Not that damn bottle," he said. "Get me a full one." I obliged and he tucked it away under the blanket and went off to the hospital in the best of spirits. He died within a few days.

Living on the premises has a lot of obvious advantages but as I soon found out, it also has one great disadvantage. Because I am always on the spot, I am always on duty, day and night, seven days a week, all the year round.

One night I had been out to dinner with some friends and returned to the house, very late, around three o'clock, with the beginnings of a raging headache. I went straight to bed and my head had hardly touched the pillow before the phone started to ring. It was one of the night security men.

"Mr. Murphy," he began, "A kangaroo has . . ."

"I know, " I said, "he's out again. Don't worry, he won't do much damage during the night. I'll get him back first thing tomorrow." I put down the phone.

I knew only too well what this was all about.

This was the period when we were removing all the railings and fences from the animal enclosures and re-placing them with dikes. It was an idea I'd picked up after a visit to Hanover Zoo. In an attractive setting like the Dublin Zoological Gardens, with only dikes separat-ing several species of wild animals, it appeared that the animals were all loose in the gardens together—camels, zebras, giraffes. It had worked very well with the zebras and camels and the giraffes, so I didn't see any reason why it should not work equally well with the kangaroos.

But you can never tell. Far from accepting the dike as their natural territorial boundary, the kangaroos regarded it much more in the light of a challenge and were forever leaping across it and wandering around the remainder of the zoo.

This didn't present much of a problem because they are harmless animals and all we had to do was chase them in the right direction and they would hop back over the dike again quite happily. During the hours we were open to the public, the presence of the visitors kept the kangaroos firmly on their side of the dike. It was only very early in the morning or late in the evening that they indulged in this game of leaping the dike. One fellow in particular was an absolute devil; a most persistent individual. I had been called out of my bed to deal with him several times before, but this particular night it was very late and I had a bad headache so I decided to allow him his freedom until the morning.

The phone rang again. It was the night security man, as I knew it would be. A most inconveniently conscientious character. "Mr. Murphy," he said, "I'm sorry to have to disturb you again, sir. But that kangaroo . . ."

Again I cut him short. "Leave him loose in the zoo grounds and I'll get him first thing in the morning."

"But Mr. Murphy, I'm trying to tell you . . . He isn't in the zoo grounds at all. He's away off down the Circular Road, heading for the city centre."

The North Circular Road is a busy main road, even at night. I had visions of some unfortunate individual driving along and suddenly seeing a kangaroo hopping past. As likely as not the poor man would be so shocked he might wrap his car around a lamp post.

Rubbing the sleep out of my eyes, I outlined the

plan of campaign. The security man had already called out the other night watchman, which was a great help, and they both had vans. I suggested that they get to either end of the road and then drive towards each other. That way they would trap the kangaroo between them and I'd be along myself immediately.

It was a curious sight: in the dead of night, on a major road, was the Director of the Dublin Zoo with a tuxedo pulled over his pyjamas, half asleep. Drawn up across the road were two security vans with their headlights on. In between them, hopping around as happy as Larry, was the kangaroo, seemingly quite undisturbed by the strange surroundings and the bright lights. It looked like an extremely sinister ambush.

When it came to the crunch, catching him presented no problem at all. He let me get close to him, civilly enough, and before he had time to realize what was happening, I had grabbed him by the tail. Powerful as they can be, kangaroos are helpless if you get them by the tail and hold on tight. You can do the same with quite big lion and tiger cubs, though obviously not once they are fully-grown. The whole secret is to keep the pressure on.

We had the kangaroo back in his enclosure inside ten minutes.

But I'd learnt another lesson. You can't go on indefinitely trying to keep kangaroos confined behind a dike if they decide otherwise. So now the visitors to the zoo have to view our splendid collection of marsupials through a wire mesh fencing.

We are constantly experimenting, trying to find new ways of exhibiting the animals.

The animals keep experimenting too, in their own way, particularly the monkeys and apes.

I decided to transfer our troop of rhesus monkeys into the old bear pit—the original bear pit of my childhood days in fact—a type of enclosure very common in old zoos. It didn't really suit the bears at all and it was not good from the public's point of view because it meant looking down on the animals from above, which gives a misleading idea of their size and shape. People leaned over the parapet and threw buns and apples down at the bears who responded by catching whatever was going with surprising agility for such clumsy-looking animals.

I moved the bears to fresh quarters and reconstructed the pit to suit the monkeys. A castle-like structure was built in the centre for the monkeys to climb on. The castle came right up to the top of the pit, which was about seventeen feet deep, but there was a gap of about twenty-four feet between the top of the castle and the parapet of the surrounding wall—a big enough gap, you would imagine, to discourage a relatively small monkey like a rhesus from attempting to leap across it. To be doubly sure, though, we placed a live electric wire around the very top of the pit which would give the monkeys a slight shock if they ever got that close to freedom.

When we first put the monkeys into their new home, they tried for a few days to get out by scampering up the outer wall at top speed, but they could never build up sufficient momentum to make it to the top, and eventually gave that up as a bad job and settled in quite happily. We sat back happily too, convinced that at least this experiment had proved a complete success. The animals seemed extremely content scrambling all over their castle, there were relatively few fights between them, and the visitors too seemed delighted with the new arrangement.

Then one day, without any warning, one of the rhesus monkeys quite casually vaulted across the gap between the top of the castle and the parapet. Within a matter of minutes, the rest of the troop had followed him.

I suppose they work on the same principle as we do: what man has done, man can do. Naturally I didn't have much opportunity for such philosophical musings at the time, with twenty-two extremely active and agile monkeys on the loose and swarming all over the gardens.

The first monkey had, ironically, used the very device I had installed to keep them in to help him get out. He had jumped on to the electric wire and the shock he received thrust him onwards, and over the parapet. The others took precisely the same route.

They were everywhere: in the kitchens, in the restaurant, scampering over the tables, swinging out of the electric light bulbs, knocking over the afternoon tea-cups. They were in the Parrot House, pestering the life out of the parrots, who were screeching in terror; they invaded the public toilets, raising startled screams from the occupants who didn't expect their privacy at such a moment to be so rudely disturbed by a troop of monkeys. They got into the offices; they got on to the roofs of other cages, driving the animals hysterical; they shinned up the drainpipes onto the roof of the house; and some of them climbed the zoo perimeter railings and went on the rampage in Phoenix Park. It was total pandemonium.

Also, although we didn't realize it at the time, a few of them had got clear of Phoenix Park altogether and were heading for the city.

There is one, simple, golden rule in the zoo—no matter what happens, all zoo personnel must keep calm —or at any rate, appear calm. One must always walk and never run, unless it is absolutely essential, and behave as if everything is under perfect control. This is re-assuring both to the public and to the animals. But on this occasion, I must admit, there was a fair bit of running about and the atmosphere we created was far from one of inner calm and confidence.

Before long we had managed to net the monkeys which had gone into the various zoo houses and buildings. A few of the more adventurous spirits were trickier to recapture but eventually, by about seven o'clock, and none the worse for a few nips, we could report: ALL QUIET IN THE DUBLIN ZOO.

Nine monkeys, however, were still unaccounted for, and stories started to percolate in from the outside world. One had been spotted in the Military Barracks on Infirmary Road. Another had been seen swiping a string of sausages from the kitchens of the official residence of the President of Ireland.

By nightfall, reports were starting to reach us that some of the monkeys had invaded a housing estate in Cabra, a nearby Dublin suburb, where they were breaking into the kitchens and stealing food. Basically rhesus monkeys are not dangerous, but if unsuspecting children tried to stroke them or play with them while they were engaged in the deadly serious business of stealing food, there was always the chance that the children could get a nasty nip. The police began to get anxious and started pressuring us to get them all back inside the zoo before they were obliged to intervene.

For the next few days we were kept busy. Every now and then we'd hear reports that a monkey had been seen and we'd pile into cars with nets, and bananas to use as bait, and go off hunting. As often as not it would turn out to be a false alarm, sometimes a genuine mistake, sometimes a hoax. Whenever we managed to track one down, we'd try to manoeuvre it into a room somewhere then close all the doors and windows and go in with a net.

By the end of the week there was only one still at

large and we kept getting reports from the Cabra estate that he was persistently breaking into kitchens, raiding larders and frightening the life out of the children.

By now, the police were threatening to shoot him. I decided that if one of my monkeys was to be shot, I'd rather do the job myself.

I eventually tracked him down and approached him in a final attempt to capture him alive; he shinned up a drainpipe and sat defying me on the roof ridge of one of the houses. I did everything in my power to lure him down peaceably but by this time he'd been on the loose for a full week, and paid no attention to me. This was before the days of the tranquillizer gun and I had no option but to shoot him.

The experiment in the bear pit eventually turned out to be a total success. We removed the electric wire and the rhesus monkeys never tried to escape again.

Another species of animal that often manages to go out on the town is the raccoon. Raccoons are small nocturnal animals, related to the bear family, and originating from North America. It is from their fur that Davy Crockett hats are made. They are extremely good swimmers and climbers—two talents which come in handy when you decide to go in for escapes.

They are also very restless, inquisitive creatures, always looking for a way out of their cage or enclosure, always on the search for some little crack or crevice to enlarge and turn into an escape route. They are well known as larder-raiders in Canada and the United States, and with front paws rather like human hands, they are adept at getting into dustbins and hen runs.

We had three of them escape together and it was three weeks before we got them all back.

The first report we had was that one had been seen

on the platform of what was then Westland Row Railway Station, right in the centre of the city. Eventually, and appropriately enough, we picked him up from the Lost Property Office.

The second one turned up a week later in Schoolhouse Lane, not far away from the Shelbourne Hotel and the Government Buildings. I went there and found him in excellent shape, living on the top floor of a semi-derelict building. He had travelled right across the city, scavenging his way along and living on the contents of dustbins.

The third one came back of his own accord after three weeks; we discovered him sitting disconsolately on top of his cage one morning, more or less begging to be allowed back home and he seemed overjoyed to rejoin his two friends in captivity.

One evening the matron of a nearby hospital rang me to say that she had seen an animal in the hospital grounds which could have been a dog but looked to her far more like a wild animal. She suggested that it might be one of my coyotes. At first I didn't believe her because I was not aware that a coyote was on the loose and I didn't think anybody who was not an animal expert could possibly tell a coyote from, say, an Alsatian at a quick glance. But I checked and found that, sure enough, there was one coyote missing. So I rang her back and asked if she had any further information. She told me that she had just phoned down to the man at the gate and asked him whether he had seen anything resembling a coyote entering the hospital premises. He'd certainly seen it but had thought it was a rather peculiar dog.

I drove to the hospital and found the coyote hiding at the back of one of the toilets. Once again, catching him was not as great a problem as you might think. As with kangaroos and small cats the trick is to catch the tail and hold on tight, so that there's no way the animal can turn around and snap at you.

Our keepers are very good at handling animals that try to escape and usually get them back without any great panic. A keeper called Gerry was passing beside the lion enclosure one day, where we had a pride with five cubs about nine months old, when he noticed that the cubs had found a weak spot in the wire and had got out. They were about the size of large dogs though both heavier and stronger. There is an outer wire beyond their enclosure so the people around did not notice that the cubs were in an area where they shouldn't be, but it would not have been any trouble at all for them to break through the outer wire and go on the loose. The mother and father were both dozing inside the inner enclosure.

Instead of sounding the alarm and creating instant panic, Gerry simply treated the lion cubs as if they were dogs and coolly shooed all five of them back through the opening they'd made in the wire fencing and fixed it up.

Mind you, we were lucky. Had the cubs been a few months older they might well have turned and attacked him. Also, they had reached an age at which the mother was beginning to lose interest in them. If they had been any younger she would certainly have noticed their absence immediately and would have followed them out through the gap, and then we'd have had a really serious problem on our hands. But there's no doubt that in this instance it was Gerry's composure that did the trick.

On other occasions it isn't composure or tact that is required but brute force.

Take for instance the first time the elephant seal escaped. These are massive creatures, weighing at least a couple of tons when fully grown. The one that escaped ate ninety pounds of herrings a day even though he was still a youngster. It cost the best part of £1,400 a year to feed him but fortunately he had been sponsored by the Irish Fisheries Board.

This elephant seal had flopped up to the edge of his enclosure and leaned on the four-foot iron railings. They bent over with his weight. We never imagined he had either the energy or the initiative to get over the top.

We were wrong, of course. One day he was seen waddling along one of the side roads in the gardens. Luckily it was fairly late in the day so there were plenty of keepers around. Also, he was comparatively young and easy to handle. They simply got a large tarpaulin, lured him on to it by offering him some fish and then, catching hold of the edge of the tarpaulin, dragged him back to his enclosure as if he were on a sleigh. He seemed to enjoy the ride, but it took the full strength of twelve tough keepers to provide the necessary power to get him over the railings again.

The next time he escaped it was a different matter altogether. By now he was fully grown—over fifteen feet in length—and weighed over two tons. I was making my early morning rounds—on this occasion in my car as it was a dull, drizzly day—and as I drove around a corner, I saw this enormous animal hobbling along the path as if he owned the place. I turned the car around immediately and raced back to the main zoo buildings where I collected a bucket of fish with which I hoped to tempt him back to his enclosure. I returned on foot. He was in a particularly aggressive mood and not in the slightest bit inclined to allow himself to be hand fed. Every time I approached him with the bucket he went for me. I knew I could run a great deal faster than he could lope after me but clearly I was getting nowhere. I threw him the fish, bucket and all, but he just ran his great canines through the bucket, squashed the fish and stood there, looking at me.

On my own there was no hope of getting him under control. So I just stood there, at a safe distance, keeping him under observation.

When eventually some of the staff arrived, we tried to get him to move using broom handles: no luck. We tried tempting him with more fish; he was not interested. The nearest enclosure was the Giraffe House, so I decided that we would keep the giraff in their stables for the moment, take down a section of their outdoor paddock and try to get him in there before the public arrived. We could then decide on our next move at leisure.

The keepers started to put the plan into effect immediately. A large section of the railings around the outer giraffe enclosure was removed and we began to move him towards this using brooms and garden implements of all kinds plus a builder's dumper truck, for which he seemed to show a certain amount of healthy respect.

Within an hour we had him safely inside the giraffe enclosure and had replaced the railings. For the moment he was safe, and so were the public. But what to do next? We had the original crate in which he had arrived at the zoo, so we got that out and put it into the giraffe enclosure with him.

Two problems now faced us. One: how to induce him to re-enter the crate—by now a very tight fit. And two: how to move a crate containing a two-ton animal (always assuming we were successful in achieving phase one) from the giraffe enclosure to his own one, right beside the sea-lion pond.

I telephoned the public transport company and explained my predicament. They said that if we could manage to get the animal back into his crate, they could provide a mobile crane capable of transporting him from one side of the gardens to the other.

The dumper truck provided the answer to the first problem. We gradually manoeuvred him into his crate, literally shovelling him along with the truck's scoop under his rear. As soon as we had him safely secured in his crate, the transport people came along with a mobile crane powerful enough to hoist the crate over the high railings of the giraffe paddock and carry him back to his own quarters.

There have been only one or two occasions when an animal has escaped and its absence has not been noticed immediately. I well remember the day when two Canadian bears managed, somehow, to escape from their enclosure and took a leisurely stroll through the gardens. The keepers and I only found out about it because Kay happened to be doing a little gardening at the time.

As she was pruning some roses near the fence of our private garden she could hear two old ladies chatting on the main drive that leads from the entrance into the zoo.

"What I love about this zoo," one of them remarked casually to the other, "is the way the animals are allowed the freedom to roam around the grounds."

Kay's head shot up and she peered over the fence to find out exactly what they were talking about. Further up the drive were the two bears—romping along quite merrily. Kay dashed indoors and raised the alarm. These bears were reasonably tame as wild bears go, but that's not saying a great deal. Within seconds a whole posse of keepers was after them and the two old ladies wandered off rather bemused.

When the bears found themselves surrounded, they obligingly climbed up into a tree. I say obligingly because once they were up there, we knew we had them. They would not come down as long as there were keepers standing guard under the tree, so it was simply a question of fetching a ladder and sending a man up the tree to a higher point than the branch on which the bears were huddled. He forced them down and we had them in boxes and on their way back to their quarters in a matter of minutes.

Bears can show a considerable amount of ingenuity at times. We moved our two little Malayan sun bears into a spanking new enclosure which they proceeded to wreck. Young bears are extremely destructive. Having done their worst to the logs and poles and bushes they attacked the concrete and succeeded in finding a weak spot. A keeper watched with considerable curiosity as one of the bears kept emerging from behind a bush carrying stones and earth in his paws. He couldn't see where the other one was. On closer investigation we found that they were actually co-operating with one another in digging a tunnel. One of them was busy scraping and as soon as he had loosened sufficient stones and earth he gathered the rubble in his paws and passed it over to the second bear who then carried it to another part of the enclosure.

With animals trying to tunnel their way to freedom I felt like an officer in charge of a prisoner of war camp, and with highly ingenious inmates. But, I'm glad to say the bears soon settled down quite peaceably and made no further escape attempts.

A spider monkey—just hanging about.

The thick iron bars and cages of days gone by *left* have now been replaced by glass-fronted indoor compartments *above* and large, open enclosures outside.

Duikers are tiny antelopes and the baby is no larger than a rabbit. This mother gave birth after a Caesarian operation.

above Bar-headed geese George and Liza stroll towards the lake with their goslings.
left A Capuchin monkey high in the trees on one of the islands.

These coins, keys, sticks
and a large lump of coal
right were all found in
the stomach of a dead
ostrich.

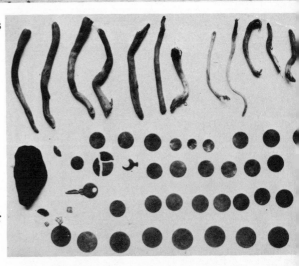

opposite King penguins
on the look out for their
keeper—it must be
feeding time.

Flamingoes by the lake—the tiny chick *opposite* was the first to be
successfully hatched at the zoo. These elegant birds remain calm
as two gulls squabble over their food *above*.

above A beautiful Mandarin duck.

opposite A cockatoo.

Our massive elephant seal was always highly
co-operative at feeding time but when he escaped
only a dumper truck could persuade him to move
towards his crate.

In one end . . . and straight out the other! Hilda the hippopotamus entered her crate one day to go on a journey *opposite* but to our astonishment she emerged through the other end having parted the thick iron bars which stood in her way.

An American black bear with her cub.

Animals About The House

MY HOME WAS right in the middle of the zoo in more ways than one—it often looked like an animal house inside. Before we had a permanent animal hospital I would always bring an animal indoors if it looked sickly and would keep it in a box or cage in the kitchen. The open-range cooker ensured that it was always warm and comfortable there. At first Kay was hostile to the idea. Apart from all the extra trouble the animals caused, she had never been used to anything more savage than the Siamese cats we bred in Blackhorse Avenue.

This is not strictly true. She did once have an unfortunate experience with a wild animal—a very tiny, indigenous one—while we were living in the bungalow. It was an orphaned Irish stoat—a baby, no bigger than six inches long—which had been brought in by a visitor to the zoo. I decided to rear it in our kitchen. It seemed tame and settled in with us very amicably.

One day I was in my office at the zoo when Kay phoned. She complained that the stoat was attacking her.

"Attacking you?" I said. "But it's no more than six inches long. How could it possibly attack you? Shoo it away back into its box."

"Terry, you won't believe this, but I've been afraid of that thing ever since you brought it into the house. I don't like the way it looks at me. It has a peculiar look in its eye right now and it's coming straight at me and I've only got these flimsy sandals on and . . . Terry! It's going for my toe! You'll have to come and rescue me!"

She was almost hysterical so I drove back home immediately.

When I got there I found Kay standing on a chair in the kitchen with the stoat staring up at her, menacingly. For some reason the stoat seemed to have taken a deep dislike to Kay. As soon as I called him, he came trotting over to me as pally as a puppy dog. But needless to say, I had to find a new home for him.

Later, when we started taking lion and tiger cubs into the house and keeping them there until they were really far too big, she never turned a hair and would handle them as casually as she would a docile Labrador. But small animals like stoats and mice, and above all snakes, still terrify her. She will occasionally allow a snake to be draped around her neck for publicity photographs but always under heavy protest.

My suggestion that we should take a lion cub into the house and hand rear him elicited the first protest.

"Terry," she said. "There's no way I'm going to have a wild animal like that in this house."

The "wild animal" she was talking about was Sampson, a pathetic little weakling of a lion cub only about ten inches long which had been deserted by its mother. A delightful little creature, as I tried to explain to Kay.

"It'll go for Pooh-bah," she argued. "It'll probably devour him."

But our Pekinese had the advantage of age and experience. Our house was Pooh-bah's territory and no sick or baby animal, however big it was, would dare take on a spritely little adult dog on that dog's home ground.

Of course, as I knew she would, Kay agreed to allow Sampson to join us in the house. He was tiny and weak, and from the moment he arrived, Pooh-bah was established in the cub's mind as the dominant animal around the place and Sampson respected him as such. While the cub was small, Pooh-bah could easily dominate him but even when Sampson grew to be several times the size of the dog, Pooh-bah remained the boss.

Sampson lived in a tiny pen, rather like a child's play pen, which I had built especially for him. We had to have something with bars around it so that we could feed him with ease. You cannot hold a baby lion for long periods because the perspiration on human hands rubs the fine fur off the cub, and it takes some time to grow again. Consequently it is best to feed them where they are relaxed and comfortable, avoiding human contact.

It was a full-time job, rearing that cub, mainly because he was the first baby wild cat we had hand-reared. Kay and I spent hours with him, and Pooh-bah was usually close at hand, casting a watchful eye over the proceedings.

When Sampson wet himself he responded in precisely the same way as a baby, not liking the sensation of a damp behind. He cried, or should I say howled. In the wild, or the lion's enclosure, the mother will immediately lick the cub until it is dry and comfortable again. We could not use a towel because of rubbing away that fine fur, but eventually Kay had a brilliant idea.

"Try my hair-dryer. Surely that will work."

I lifted his tail and played the jet of warm air gently over his hindquarters. Soon all was peace and quiet and Sampson was purring like a contented kitten.

We kept Sampson with us until he was four months old and we were very sad when he left permanently for the zoo proper. We continued to take him for walks for a while after that, when he was as tall as a Great Dane and a lot heavier, with enormous paws. Pamela, a young secretary at the zoo, often took him out on a lead and he never gave her a single anxious moment. He was fine with anyone who knew how to handle him.

But it was impossible to keep him in the house any longer. Lions, or any big cats, do not suddenly grow vicious or turn on you, it's simply that they grow too big to manage and they can do an enormous amount of damage about the house with their claws and teeth.

They can also be rather too boisterously affectionate. If they become excited and throw themselves at you, you're lucky to escape with only dislocated bones. Sampson ripped the clothes off my back on several occasions when I was playing with him. I was prepared for all this but we had our visitors to consider.

One morning the vacuum cleaner repairman dropped by. Sampson, always highly inquisitive, especially if people came to the house, bounded out into the hall. The repairman stared in horror as Sampson leaped towards him—intending to welcome him, no more. Our visitor turned white and bolted. On another occasion the Australian Ambassador to Ireland, a friend of ours, was greeted with such enthusiasm that he was knocked down the the stairs by Buster, a tiger cub whom we kept for far too long.

So Sampson had to go into an enclosure and eventually, as a huge, healthy, adult lion, he went to another zoo.

Dublin Zoo has always had a great reputation for breeding lions but breeding tigers was far more difficult. When Arja, a magnificent tigress, gave birth to four healthy cubs but then rejected them, I decided immediately to take them into our house. Kay was understandably concerned at the prospect.

"One lion cub—all right," she said. "We've proved that we can handle that one. But four tiger cubs. I just haven't got enough hands."

She had a point. It really wouldn't have been possible for Kay and myself to devote all the care and attention that we'd lavished on Sampson to four tiger cubs, however attractive and appealing they might have been. If these cubs survived they would be the first tiger cubs ever to be reared in Dublin Zoo. I was already very proud of them and absolutely determined to do all in my power to save them.

I put out an appeal on the radio for foster parents for them. The response was enormous and immediate. We chose two beautiful collie dogs, Flossie and Dolly, who were nursing pups of their own. The collie puppies and the little tigers got along famously and Flossie and Dolly didn't seem to find anything unusual or odd about nursing a couple of tiger cubs among their own offspring. The experiment went very well, even though our kitchen was overflowing with baby animals.

They grew up fast and we were soon facing the same problems as we had with Sampson—only this time multiplied by four. Apart from sharpening their claws on the furniture, eating cushions, and bounding about the house knocking everything flying, including any human beings who got in the way, their favourite pastime was climbing the venetian blinds. To the cubs they appeared eminently fascinating. They tried to clamber up them as if the blinds were ladders and of course they collapsed, sending a heap of twisted metal and baffled feline crashing to the floor.

All four tigers were strong and healthy when we transferred them into an enclosure. I couldn't wait to announce to the press that at long last we had succeeded in breeding tigers in Dublin Zoo and to present our four young celebrities to the world.

When the big day came, all the newspaper, television and radio people turned up. Because the cubs were so accustomed to human contact, I allowed our visitors to handle them. It was all terrific publicity, but a tragic mistake on my part.

Unknown to us all, one of the people who held the cubs had a cat which was suffering from feline enteritis. As the cat's owner caressed and played with them, the cubs were contracting the infection. Within forty-eight hours all four were dead.

It was one of the saddest moments of my life.

No one should have been allowed to touch those animals before they had been inoculated against all possible infections. I had learned a bitter lesson.

I felt totally responsible for their death but I must stress that this occurrence should not be taken as an argument against rearing animals in captivity. In a zoo, the mortality rate for, say, lion cubs, is no more than ten per cent. In the wild that mortality rate is far, far higher. And today, zoos must be the safest place on earth for an animal to give birth. With such facilities as special maternity units, two-way radios, closed-circuit television, incubators and under-floor heating in the enclosures, a baby animal receives almost as much attention as a baby human being. I feel very proud to have been with the Dublin Zoo during its most progressive period. For well over a hundred years the zoo was static and unchanging. Today it is transformed and I feel privileged to have been able to play my part in that transformation.

Our kitchen is no longer the sanctuary for sick or rejected baby animals; they now go to the hospital unit. No longer do we place half-dead baby animals in a tin lined with cotton wool and then place it in a slow oven hoping it will revive. No longer does Kay have to work in the kitchen, taking care not to disturb a tiny bird in a cardboard box on top of the cooker, with bouncy cubs playing between her legs, and an otter creating havoc in the broom cupboard, while Pooh-bah desperately tries to keep a semblance of order in the place.

But even in those days, in the somewhat makeshift conditions of our kitchen, the baby animals were extremely well looked after. It was the usual occupants of the house who often had a raw deal. Both Kay and Pooh-bah rebelled at times when I became over-confident about the sort of animals we could care for. Kay was always tolerant and calm—until I brought home the camel.

It had been born in the middle of the most dreadful storm—trees crashed to the ground in Phoenix Park, slates were hurled from rooftops and the wind howled across the zoo. The mother camel had been terrified and was far too upset to cope with her child so I took the newborn creature to our kitchen.

Kay was furious. Quite apart from the fact that we had rather a large number of animal guests at the time, that newborn creature was three feet six inches high and built rather like a baby foal with a hump on its back. Kay was right—it was far too big to be accommodated in our home, so we sent it back to the camel's enclosure where the keeper took good care of it.

Pooh-bah was rather intolerant of another creature —Joey the kangaroo. I had taken Joey in because his mother seemed unable to feed him properly. He took very well to hand-rearing and grew at an enormous rate. He followed me everywhere, taking a whole flight of stairs in two bounds and often jumping on to or over the found Joey rather difficult though.

As they were play, Joey would suddenly take a great leap and utterly vanish out of Pooh-bah's field of vision. The peke could never figure this out, especially as Joey usually came into view again several yards away. Pooh-bah didn't trust Joey one bit and only tolerated him at all because he was accepted by both Kay and myself.

There was another of our house guests who gave Pooh-bah rather a hard time but I do not think in this case that Pooh-bah was aware of the cause of his confusion.

Percy the parrot lived in a cage in my office, on the ground floor of our home, for many years. He and I were the best of friends. But whenever I went out of the office and left him alone, Percy would get upset. However, he had his ways of getting me to return.

He had learned to imitate the buzz of my internal phone with great skill—hardly surprising since he practised all day. He would also imitate me answering the phone. As soon as I settled down with a book upstairs, or was about to tuck into my lunch, I'd hear the buzz of the phone from my office.

Down I would dash, well aware that it was probably Percy, but it sounded so exactly like the zoo's internal telephone system that I couldn't afford to take any chances. More often than not there would be no reply to my "Hello" as I picked up the receiver, and as I walked out of the office in a huff I'd often hear a mocking impersonation of my own voice from behind me: "Hello, yes . . ." And then Percy would be seized with a fit of hysterical screeching as if well pleased at his own joke.

He nearly drove poor Pooh-bah mad. He would imitate my voice and my whistle perfectly. Hearing what he took to be me whistling for him to go for a walk, Pooh-bah would go scampering down to the office only to find that it was empty—except for Percy.

There were times when Percy would call Kay in my voice and then call me in her voice, and then scream "Pooh-bah, Pooh-bah" until he had all three of us dashing up and down the stairs.

Another talking bird also proved to be quite a character.

One day somebody telephoned me from the Dublin docks and said that a cockatoo had turned up there and would the Dublin Zoo take it? I never find it easy to turn down an offer of a bird or an animal, so I was in my car and down at the docks within minutes.

The bird had arrived on a ship and the captain no longer wanted it on board. I put him in the back of my car and set out for home.

Suddenly a stream of oaths and blasphemies that would have blistered the paint on any door came hurtling at me from the back of the car as I drove through the city.

By the time we reached the zoo I had decided that I would be the perpetrator of a grave scandal if I put this bird on view, thus exposing decent members of the public to appalling bad language. There was nothing for it but to keep him in the house until I could find a suitable home.

He was quite tame so, in my office, I let him go free. He immediately flew to the top of the curtains and refused to come down, despite all my attempts to persuade him. He just perched up there, hurling abuse on top of my head.

You can usually get a bird, any bird, to come down off its perch by gently placing a stick under its breast:

it will move from its perch on to the stick.

I decided to try this and got hold of a broom handle. Immediately the cockatoo went berserk. "What are you doing with that stick?" he screamed, over and over again. "What are you doing with that stick?"

I was so amazed I almost began to explain what I was doing with the broom before I realized that I was responding to a cockatoo. It was the most polite utterance he'd made so far. Obviously, by sheer coincidence, that cockatoo had learned to recognize and exclaim about sticks on the ship. But for one moment it sounded as if I had acquired a bird capable of conversation!

Quite often the tiniest animals caused far more trouble about the house than the big ones. There's a rather cute creature, a ground squirrel from West Africa, with a very appealing expression—two large teeth sticking awkwardly out of his mouth and a lovely, long, bushy tail. We had one called Sydney. If I let him out of his box, he'd climb on to my shoulder and perch there as I walked around. I got nervous when he started pinching at my ears with those great incisors, but he was generally a friendly little fellow and a great house pet.

Or so I thought; until one day when he was loose in the living room and Kay suddenly shouted: "Terry, look what Sydney's doing to the carpet."

I looked. What Sydney was doing to the carpet was going through it at great speed like a combine harvester, chewing it up, spitting it out and leaving a straight furrow behind him. As Kay and I rushed towards him, he stopped and jumped up to a sitting position. He gave us one startled look, turned to glance across the room, and then in a second was away, streaking towards the legs of our best armchairs, which he proceeded to chew with great vigour.

After that performance, Sydney joined the ranks of the zoo proper very quickly indeed.

Acting as surrogate parents to neglected animals sometimes presented Kay and me with tasks we simply could not fulfil ourselves. When a female Mangabay monkey totally rejected her baby, I took the tiny creature home and we began to care for it in the normal way—feeding it by bottle, keeping it warm and comfortable, and making sure it received plenty of company and attention.

The little monkey did not respond. It became more and more distressed and remained weak. Each time we lifted it from its box it would cling to our clothes with such determination that it was quite a task to disentangle it. As soon as we returned it to its box it would whimper and pine. It became obvious that the baby monkey desperately needed someone, or something, to hold on to at all times if it was to grow normally and remain happy.

Baby Mangabays always cling to their mothers—clinging to her fur is a fundamental aspect of their early life. In the wild, the mother cannot hold the baby because she needs the use of all her limbs to swing around the trees and to make a nimble escape if anything threatens her and her child. The baby has to cling on firmly: if it does not it will lose its only source of food and comfort, and be left as easy prey for any hungry predators that may be about.

Neither I nor anyone else around the zoo, could possibly spend the whole time attached to a monkey so we had to find some alternative if this baby was going to survive. I was dubious as to whether it would work, but I thought I would try giving our Mangabay a small towel.

We'd solved the problem.

That monkey became totally attached to the towel,

both physically and emotionally. If we took the towel away to wash it, the monkey howled until he got his "mother" back. And no other piece of towelling would do.

After a few weeks the baby began to move away from the towel—at first only for a few seconds but gradually for longer and longer periods. It was behaving just as any young monkey does—moving away from its mother as it matures and going off to forage for its own food. But the towel had to be left wherever the monkey placed it because the moment the Mangabay was frightened it would dash directly to the towel for comfort.

When we returned the young Mangabay to the Monkey House, the towel went too but we had a happy, well-adjusted and confident little monkey who joined the rest without problems.

One of the things that you very quickly learn when you live among animals—and you learn it even more rapidly if you have them living in the kitchen with you—is that they all see the world from a different angle, according to their size. It helps to understand them if you put yourself in their position and try to imagine what the world must look like from their point of view.

One of our house guests was a tiny duckling. Imagine for a moment that you are a duckling with your eyes roughly four or five inches above ground level. What do you see? Feet, mainly.

I was wearing a pair of green Wellington boots when I rescued this little duckling who wasn't looking too healthy and had obviously been deserted. It soon became very attached to me—or rather to that part of me to which it could relate: my green Wellington boots. Whenever I was wearing those boots, I was followed everywhere by a tiny duckling who completely ignored me if I turned up in slippers or any other footwear.

In fact, there were times when I was feeding this dear little bird late at night and wearing slippers, and as soon as it was satisfied it would ignore me but try to snuggle up to my empty green wellies.

It gives one a sense of proportion, an incident like that. All I ever meant to that little duckling whom I found and cherished was a pair of green Wellington boots.

From A
Great Height

W E'VE BEEN LOOKING at the world from the viewpoint of a duckling. Now let's go to the other
end of the scale and try to imagine how it
looks to the lofty and graceful giraffe. Giraffes can grow
to nearly eighteen feet high so they get an aerial view
of the remainder of the animal world, including human-
ity. The distance of a giraffe's eyes from the ground helps
account for the fact that they are rather awkward animals
to keep in a zoo. This is mainly due to their size and
build. They are absolutely enormous when fully grown,
with gigantic heads on those incredibly long necks, and
their powerful bodies resting on slender legs and
relatively small hooves. Place all that in an enclosure,
remembering that they are both shy and highly inquisitive, and you can understand why we keep a watchful eye on our giraffes at all times.

Although the Dublin Zoo's international reputation
was based on its lions, it has also had a very long association with giraffes—the giraffe holds pride of place as
the emblem on the Society's tie.

As long ago as 1844, thirteen years after the Zoological Gardens were first opened to the public, the Society received the gift of a young male giraffe from the London Zoo: Albert, he was called, after his keeper. He had the distinction of being the first giraffe to be born and survive in Europe. In return, the Royal Zoological Society of Ireland presented the London Zoo with two animals never previously seen alive in England —a two-toed sloth and an unusual variety of ocelot known as *felis melanura*.

Albert grew fast; very fast and very tall. A special building had to be constructed to house him, and it was known as the Albert Tower. That building was demolished quite recently to make way for a new hippopotamus enclosure, and behind one of the cornerstones were found newspapers, documents and coins of the period when it was built—including a specially-minted coin to commemorate Albert as the first giraffe to set foot on Irish soil.

It was over half a century before a second giraffe took Albert's place in the zoo. This animal was presented in 1902 by a character called Butler Bey, a distinguished Irish officer who held an important military post in El Obeid, in the Sudan.

Butler Bey offered this giraffe to the zoo as a gift, on condition that the Society would undertake responsibility for its transport to Dublin. He did agree, however, to allow his African servant to accompany the animal to Dublin at his expense. The Council accepted Butler Bey's offer and entered into negotiations with Messrs. Thomas Cook and Company to arrange for the transportation. They insured the giraffe for £1,000—a very considerable sum in those days.

A contemporary account of the journey from Africa, still preserved in the Royal Zoological Society's files, reveals some of the problems they faced.

The party left El Obeid on May 6, 1902, on the first stage to Omdurman, a distance of 280 miles over savanna country. On this section of the journey the giraffe was obliged to walk, with six locally-recruited helpers to lead him by means of a head collar and a series of long ropes (long, presumably, to enable them to exercise control while remaining outside the range of his highly lethal hooves).

When they arrived at Omdurman, they transported the animal across the Nile to Khartoum, the capital of the Sudan. They arrived at the same time as another consignment of animals which included four giraffes. These other animals were for various European zoos and the consignment was under the personal direction of Captain Flower, director of the zoological gardens at Gizeh, near Cairo. Captain Flower had with him a large staff and readily agreed to take over the responsibility of transporting Butler Bey's giraffe to Dublin, along with Bey's servant.

Before the animals were permitted to enter Egypt, they had to undergo a twenty-one day quarantine period and were then conveyed down the Nile by a *gyhassa*, a primitive sailing boat still in use, to El Shallal, where they caught the train for Cairo.

"Caught the train" is perhaps putting it rather casually considering what was actually involved. This was a particularly hazardous part of the journey as the trains travelled under six very low bridges between El Shallal and Cairo, so all of the giraffes, (the Dublin-bound one being by far the tallest) were in grave danger of being decapitated.

The animals were accommodated in special crates which had sliding roofs through which their heads could protrude for most of the journey, but every time a bridge appeared on the horizon, a team of men undertook the task of hauling the giraffes' heads down and closing over the sliding roofs of the crates until the bridge had been safely negotiated.

The Dublin-destined animal was shipped at Alexandria on a freighter headed for Liverpool, and eventually conveyed from there to Dublin by the British and Irish Steampacket Company. The odyssey from El Obeid to Dublin had taken over three months at enormous cost both in terms of money and physical effort.

Things are a lot easier these days, but transporting giraffes is still a tricky business. In 1951, Cedric Flood and one of the keepers travelled to London to pick up three young giraffes which had been in quarantine there; they had been purchased three months earlier in East Africa and were part of a larger consignment bought for the London Zoo.

Two large, low-loading trucks took the animals from London to the Liverpool docks. The weather was severe, and on arrival in Liverpool, Cedric found that they were too late for embarkation on the Dublin boat that night so he had to find overnight accommodation for the trucks and their unusually tall cargoes. It was not easy to find a shed big enough to house three giraffes in the late evening at dead of winter. Someone thought of Speke Airport. Speke was approached, an aircraft hangar was placed at Flood's disposal, and the trucks and giraffes were parked there overnight.

The following day they continued their journey to Dublin, and I was down at the docks to meet them. They came over as deck cargo, in crates about twelve feet high, with holes cut in the top of each crate to enable the giraffes to stick their heads out and see what was going on. They are inordinately curious animals and cannot bear not knowing exactly what is happening.

We loaded them on to another truck at Dublin docks but were rather dubious about getting them under the Loop Line railway bridge that spans the Liffey. We might just have made it, but made doubly sure by letting all the air out of the tyres just before we went under the bridge. That gave us the few extra inches we needed as a safety margin. It was incredibly hard work getting those tyres back up to their correct pressure on the far side.

The three giraffes settled down very happily in Dublin and between them produced eight calves during the next few years. I was present at most of these happy events and will never forget the first of them.

We had called the giraffes Doc, Sneezy and Bashful, after the dwarfs in *Snow White*, and when Bashful became pregnant, a few years after she arrived in the zoo, we were in a bit of a dilemma because we had no experience at all in delivering giraffe calves. As we watched Bashful grow more and more pregnant, we grew more and more apprehensive about how we were going to manage at the moment of birth.

Moment of birth is rather an understatement—it went on for hours.

One lovely day in midsummer, as Bashful was calmly walking around her outer paddock, the calf's front legs appeared. Several of us stood by, keeping a good distance so as not to worry Bashful, but an hour went by and we began to get worried because the head of the calf did not appear. As with most births, the position of the baby's head is crucial and once it is out the rest of the body follows quickly and easily.

Maxi, a vet, who was an expert in delivering bloodstock foals, was called to the scene. Another hour passed, but there was still no sign of the calf's head. The vet decided it was time to give Bashful some assistance in placing the head in the right position.

She was led into her stall and the vet took charge. Using long poles with loops of rope attached to the end, we tentatively followed Bashful around the stall until we had secured the ropes on to the legs of the calf. We then got hold of the poles and pulled gently. Bashful helped by moving away from us. The person she knew best, her keeper, then approached her from behind and was able to place his hand right inside the giraffe and move the calf's head around. We continued to pull on the poles, and Bashful strained away from us. At last the head appeared—and seconds later a baby calf fell down on to the hay which had been laid across the floor of the stall.

We grinned broadly at one another—relieved and thrilled that all had gone well. But Bashful no longer wanted us around, and in a flurry of flying hooves and scrambling bodies we managed to release the loops of rope from the calf. The vet quickly threw a bucket of water over the baby to start him breathing, and we all rushed out, short of breath, rather bruised, but over-joyed.

Keeping well out of her sight, we watched Bashful gingerly approach her calf and start to lick it. Before long it had struggled to its feet and begun feeding from its mother. The calf was over five feet tall and absolutely enchanting. We named it after yet another of Snow White's dwarf friends—Happy.

When the second baby giraffe was due to be born in the zoo, we were prepared with poles, rope, a vet on hand, hay—everything. Again there was a lengthy delay after the calf first appeared but fortunately it was in completely the right position. We could see its head almost immediately. However, the mother giraffe did not give birth straight away—she merely wandered around for hours with her baby half-born. We eventually aided the birth in precisely the same way as we had with Bashful, using the ropes and poles, and again all went well.

I was somewhat puzzled as to why this birth, which should have occurred quickly because it was without complication, had taken so many hours. The calf had been in the right position, and both mother and baby were in good health. It was not until a third giraffe had been born in the zoo that we realized the delay was due to our interference.

This third birth took place in the dead of night when no one was around. The keeper discovered a healthy calf in the stall with its mother early one morning. It suddenly became clear to us that although our presence had been necessary for Bashful, it had in fact been a hindrance to the second birth. The close proximity of human beings had caused the mother to delay giving birth, just as she would in the wild if she was disturbed, or nervous that her vulnerable newborn calf could be attacked or open to anything she regarded as danger. Human beings obviously constitute a threat.

From that time on everyone has kept well out of the way when giraffes have given birth, though we now watch the proceedings on closed-circuit television in case they need assistance.

Giraffes are the only animals we insure. The premium is about fifteen per cent per annum of the value we put upon the animal. At the moment, we value them at around £2,500–£3,000 each and we get the equivalent of a no claims bonus if all goes well. We insure them not because they are so valuable—we have several species in the zoo which are far more valuable: elephants, gorillas and clouded leopards, for example—but because they are so accident-prone in captivity. For although they take very readily to captivity, they are always in trouble.

One of our giraffes managed to strangle himself.

It happened when the public and the keepers had all gone home as the giraffe attempted to get at the food in the next enclosure. He put his full weight on the railings dividing the two stalls, causing a gap to appear in the junction between the front and side railings. He was quick to take advantage of this gap and shoved his neck through it, to grab some food from the bin next door. Unfortunately, when he took his weight off the railings, the gap closed on his neck and the next morning we found him dead. It was not something that we could possibly have foreseen, though once it had happened, we were able to make sure it never occurred again. We have now arranged the railings in such a way that a giraffe, putting his weight on any rail, cannot possibly cause a gap to appear. I wish we could anticipate things such as this but there is really no way of knowing what animals are capable of doing until they actually do it.

We had another giraffe that fell into the dike—or maybe was pushed into it by one of its companions.

Originally the giraffes were housed in a paddock behind very high railings. But we replaced railings with dikes wherever possible so that people walking through the zoo would get the impression that some of the wild animals were wandering free in the pleasant surroundings of Phoenix Park. I very much wanted the elegant giraffes to be a part of this.

There was another reason why I wanted to remove the railings. When we had giraffes separated from the public only by high railings, they would be forever leaning over and taking food from people; and this was dangerous. You can lose a lot of animals from the wrong food or even too much of the right food.

I did my best to try to make our visitors realize this by putting up notices. I also stressed the problem during television programmes I appeared on—the programmes got excellent ratings but nobody paid the slightest attention to the request not to feed the animals.

I can understand why. When you have, say, ten thousand people wandering around the gardens on a public holiday, they all want to establish some sort of personal relationship with the animals, however tenuous. There is only one way of doing that—by offering them tasty food. We had to try to house the animals in such a way that the public simply could not feed them: either behind glass, or on the other side of a dike or double fence which would keep them at a safe distance.

When I replaced the railings around the giraffe enclosure with a dike I ran a wire around the perimeter just inside the dike—a single strand about five feet above the ground and strung from a series of poles. This was simply to stop them falling into the new dike. When we let the animals out they went cautiously towards the edge of their new enclosure, encountered the wire and accepted it as their new boundary. After a few weeks we were able to take this wire down since by this time they had become completely conditioned to the existence of the dike as the final boundary of their territory. I was delighted to find that they made no attempt to lean across the dike to get food from the public—the transition seemed a total success.

Then one morning we found one of the giraffes down in the dike. Nobody had any idea how he had got there. The important thing was to get him out in one piece. We climbed down into the dike and tried to edge him towards one end where there was a gentle slope. If we would get him to walk up that, we could open the gate at the top of the slope and let him back into the enclosure.

Things did not go quite so smoothly. Every time

he came close to the slope, with keepers and helpers encouraging him along, he would suddenly turn and bolt back to the centre of the dike.

We decided to solve this by blocking his retreat with a plank of wood which was placed across the dike with two men standing on either end of it. Again the giraffe was led towards the slope, again he turned and ran back, and again he got back to the middle of the dike, only this time smashing the plank in the process and sending the four men flying.

There was no point in trying to use another plank. He was clearly very upset by something down there and no plank was going to stop him running away.

I studied the dike carefully near the slope and saw that there was a pipe, about a foot above the ground, running right across the dike just before the slope. I realized that if I were a giraffe, looking down on this from about twenty feet, and that if I'd already fallen down into the dike, I'd be extremely nervous about stepping over a pipe even a mere foot above ground level, in case I fell again.

As it was a water pipe there was no way we could remove it. We fetched some sand and covered it up so that he could walk across it without having to step over it —without even seeing it in fact. It worked beautifully.

He allowed himself to be gently hustled toward the slope and climbed out of the dike without any assistance from us.

We had another young male called Patrick who died in the most unfortunate of circumstances. We had brought him from Bristol Zoo hoping that he would breed with two females we had at the time, Sinead and Sheena. Poor Patrick was found early one morning in February 1971, flat out on the floor. He resisted all the efforts of the keepers to get him back on his feet again and died in a very short time. A post-mortem examination revealed that he had a dislocated neck, and the general consensus of opinion was that he had been attempting to mate with one of the female giraffes and had fallen in the process, injuring his neck irreparably on the railings.

After Patrick's mating misadventure, my friend Jimmy Chipperfield—a member of the famous British circus family who are now involved in safari parks— agreed to sell us one of his breeding male giraffes called Jock, a very attractive animal.

Chipperfield's youngest son John was in charge of transport arrangements and decided that the most convenient method of conveying this large giraffe, which came originally from Uganda, would be by car ferry to Northern Ireland and then by road to Dublin. The year was 1971 and the authorities were keeping a close look-out for consignments of smuggled arms or indeed any-thing suspicious going across the border between the Republic and Northern Ireland.

Jock was in a vast crate built on to the chassis of a four wheel trailer and John was towing this trailer with a land rover. In order to protect the animal during the journey, a green tarpaulin had been fastened over the crate, completely concealing the giraffe.

The drive was uneventful until they reached the border. Here they were stopped and John was informed that owing to the height of the crane, he would not be able to use the main Dublin road it it passed under two low bridges. Instead John would have to travel to Dublin using minor roads.

John found that trying to navigate along narrow, unlit roads on a dark evening slowed him down con-siderably. He was beginning to get nervous about the giraffe when, to his relief, the lights of Dublin appeared ahead.

Then, out of the dark, he saw a car parked right across the road. Braking as gently as he could he pulled to a halt. Two men appeared in his headlights and approached the land rover with extreme care. John's heart thumped, knowing his vehicle looked decidedly military in appearance, especially with the tarpaulin over the crate. He thought he was about to be the victim of an ambush. As the men reached the land rover they flashed torches inside the vehicle and on to John's face. He lowered the window.

"We're police officers, son. Jump down."

John smiled at them in relief, and co-operated fully as they searched him and examined his driving licence.

"Would you mind telling me exactly what you have in the back there," one of them asked.

John continued to smile. "Not at all," he said. "It's a giraffe."

"Oh yes. A giraffe, eh. Having a little joke are you son? Well you can wipe that grin off your face because we haven't got time to stand around here listening to your funny stories. Now, for the last time, what's in that trailer?"

"A giraffe. I know it sounds ridiculous but . . ."

"Oh, he says he knows it sounds ridiculous," the policeman said turning to his companion. "He must take us for a pair of fools. Go round and take a look will you."

"Oh, let me," John exclaimed. "They're very shy animals, you might make it panic."

"You just stay right where you are, young fellow."

The second officer disappeared. John could hear him untying the tarpaulin. Then he let out a yell. "It's a giraffe!" He came rushing back. "It really *is* a giraffe."

"Are you sure?" said the first one. "A giraffe?"

"It's for the Dublin . . ." John was cut short.

"Just a moment," the policeman continued. "I want to see this for myself."

The first policeman disappeared and was back in seconds.

"It really is a giraffe!"

Obviously, the land rover and trailer had been reported to the police. It must have looked suspicious, particularly taking the back roads. By the time John finally reached the zoo, at around midnight, I was very worried because I had expected him hours earlier.

I rushed up to meet him, and noticed there was a car immediately behind the trailer.

"Who's that?" I asked John.

"Oh, it's the police escort. They insisted. I'll just go and say goodbye to them."

He jumped down from his land rover and ran round to the other car. He came back as the car zoomed away.

"Police escort? Why? And how come you're so late?"

I was bewildered.

"Let's unload the giraffe, then I'll tell you the whole story," John said, grinning.

Elephants are the only other animals of comparable size to giraffes and although they are not so accident prone they are difficult animals to care for if only because of their vast bulk.

They are highly adaptable creatures and can be trained either to work, as they do in the forests of India, or to perform tricks. Outside the old Elephant House there was a sort of circus ring of heavy bars through which visitors would feed the elephants with potatoes. In return the animal would perform a few basic tricks such as mounting a concrete pedestal and raising its trunk and legs at the bidding of his keeper. One also managed to play the mouth organ—a highly popular diversion for our visitors.

When the new house was built we used those heavy bars as part of the barrier with a dike. The space where the ring had once stood was filled in and concreted over. In those days the elephants gave rides—a practice we have since stopped for several reasons and not least because it can be dangerous.

Every afternoon when she'd finished giving her day's ration of rides Sarah the elephant would be as anxious to return to her stall as any horse is after its early morning canter. Although the ring had been removed and Sarah could easily have walked straight to the door of her stable, she always made her way very carefully around the edge of the now non-existent ring, as she had always done in the past. She would then follow her old route, walking through what was once the site of the entrance to the ring and then across to her stall.

Elephants, like giraffes, are very wary about where they put their feet; they have to be, because there's a lot of weight there, concentrated on the relatively small area represented by the soles of four feet, and it could be that she continued to take the old route because she knew from experience that the ground there was perfectly safe for walking on.

This theory might well be borne out by the fact that when the new elephant house was built we had great difficulty in persuading Sarah to walk across to the new house. It took us hours. She had never been in this area before, and the ground had been broken up by the builders. She felt her way along, very gingerly, step by step. However, once she had satisfied herself that the ground *was* perfectly safe, we never had any trouble moving her again.

Sarah was always a docile animal—very easy to control—and she never caused us any problems, even allowing the young and inexperienced Terry Murphy, on that memorable day at the start of my career, to re-move that splinter of glass from her foot. Thankfully, in my time at the zoo, we have not had an elephant as un-ruly and unpredictable as Sita the creature who acci-dentally killed her keeper in 1903. However, an elephant who joined Sarah when she was presented to the zoo as a gift from a member of the Society, proved to be rather difficult.

Komali was found as a baby, abandoned in a jungle in what was then Ceylon. There she was rescued by a friend of our society member. Komali was so small at the time that she was transported to the zoo at Colombo in the boot of his car—quite comfortably. From there she travelled by boat to Dublin.

When she arrived at the zoo, Sarah was only too pleased to have a new companion and they immediately took a liking to one another. But as Komali grew older, and bigger, it became clear she was not going to be as good-natured as her companion.

Elephants often use their shoulders and trunk to push who ever they are annoyed with, or fright-ened by, against a flat surface. They then use their mas-sive weight to crush their victim. If they succeed in knocking someone down when in an aggressive mood they will then stand on that person—again using their weight as their most lethal weapon. A fully-grown elephant is also quite capable of picking up a large man with its trunk, and hurling him a considerable distance.

Komali never actually hurt anyone but she did attempt to attack her keeper and his assistant on more than one occasion. The men who handle elephants learn how to avoid being pushed against walls or knocked over and elephants usually respond well to a keeper they know and respect.

Komali could be handled with relative ease by her

keeper Jimmy, even when she was angry or behaving unpredictably. It was on one of his days off that she caused us most problems. She became agitated and the assistant keeper found he could not control her by his voice alone and, using sheer force, she managed to break away from him and out into the grounds. Close by, a group of school children were enjoying a visit to the zoo. They were being led by a nun. As they turned at the sound of Komali's trumpeting, the nun rushed forward to stand in front of the children. Komali moved past them with some speed, nudging the nun as he went by and knocking the poor lady to the ground. She was not hurt but, understandably, rather shaken.

We knew that only Jimmy could handle Komali in this situation so we sent for him immediately and stood by ready to take action if he did not arrive before she carried out further attacks. Unfortunately a very interesting moving object caught her eye from across the zoo. A tractor was being used on a construction site and Komali decided to take it on. She rushed over and then stopped in front of it. The driver was petrified as Komali approached his vehicle, lowered her massive head and proceeded to turn the tractor over with one strong nudge from her forehead. The driver was dazed and astounded but unhurt, and as Komali looked around for more fun, Jimmy arrived on the scene. After Komali had performed a few playful charges away from him and a couple of trumpets of frustration, Jimmy was able to lead her calmly back to her stall where he gave her a severe reprimand for interrupting his day off and upsetting so many people. Komali looked suitably ashamed.

Ideally, I would like to have a small herd of elephants in a very large enclosure with proper stabling. If I had a big enough zoo, that's how I would arrange things. But they need grooming in captivity. They also need a lot of water. Our tap water is too cold for them; they have to be hosed down regularly with heated water, especially in winter, and this is an expensive business. They also need something to rub themselves against, just as they rub themselves against the trees in Africa, to keep their hides in good shape. But they're inclined to push over the trees in order to eat the roots, so there's no way that it would be possible to keep them among trees in the confined area of a zoo. In addition they are extremely expensive to buy and to feed, so I am afraid my notion of a herd of elephants in a natural setting in the Phoenix Park will have to remain a dream.

Bringing-Up Babies

OUSING, FEEDING AND caring for animals is an
extremely costly business. The zoo, unfortunately, has to run as a commercial concern because, in Dublin, our principal source of income is the
money paid for admissions by our visitors. A small
amount also comes in from grants, members' subscrip-
tions and restaurant receipts, but we basically rely on the
fact that we can attract visitors.

Baby animals play an important role in this respect.
Almost all young creatures are fascinating and endearing.
As soon as they are put on view to the public, photographs of them usually appear in the newspapers and it's
wonderful publicity for the zoo.

Breeding animals is also very important because it
allows us to exchange young animals for other species, so
replenishing our stock and bringing in a constant variety
of wild creatures. Zoos throughout the world keep in
contact and inform one another what animals they have
for exchange and which species they would like in return.

Occasionally animals are sold but the income from this is negligible and exchanges are more advantageous.

There are several reasons why we are far more concerned to breed rare and exotic creatures than the more common ones. Many zoos are now overbreeding animals such as lions. A zoo can only house a limited number, and can often find itself left with unwanted animals. In Dublin we have limited the breeding of our lions for some time and we try and plan carefully so that any animals we do not wish to retain in our zoo will be wanted by other zoos.

Also, it is important to remember that as more rare animals are bred in captivity, then less will be taken from the wild.

It was 1958 when we lost those four hand-reared tiger cubs from feline enteritis. Apart altogether from the deep sadness and disappointment we felt, those tiger cubs were impossible to replace at a time when funds were low, and we also suffered from the fact that we could not at some time in the future exchange them for new animals.

I waited impatiently for a sign that Arja, the tigress, was pregnant once more. Fortunately we did not have very long to wait. In May 1959, six months after her first cubs had died, Arja began to show all the signs of another impending litter. I immediately fitted a very sensitive microphone in her cage. This was linked in turn to a powerful amplifier. One loudspeaker was placed in the night security man's room and one in my study. Throughout the day the keepers kept a close eye on Arja and at night we turned on the microphone and amplifier. Tigers make little noise normally but we would know immediately if the cubs were born because mother and cubs give out a good strong cry at birth. The memory of losing those first four cubs after hand-rearing them was

strong in my mind. This time I was absolutely determined that the new litter would be reared successfully.

My study, where I placed one of the loudspeakers,
was off a landing in my house and we tested it to ensure
that any sound coming from Arja's enclosure could be
heard clearly throughout the house. Every day I turned
on the speaker when the keeper left for home and then
turned it off each morning—except one morning when I
was distracted by some other occurrence and completely
forgot.

Kay's daily help arrived that morning as usual and
began work in our kitchen. Suddenly a tremendous roar
made her drop a cup she was drying and she rushed into
the hall. She realized immediately that the noise was
coming from the study. In terror she ran back to the kitchen and locked herself in, convinced, quite understandably, that one of the big cats was in the house.

Kay arrived home from shopping a few minutes
later and as she tried to open the door which leads
into the kitchen, Mrs. Mac grabbed her.

"Thank goodness you came straight here Mrs.
Murphy. Had you gone near the study you would be
dead by now!"

"What on earth has happened?" Kay asked.

"There's a wild animal, or maybe several, roaring
and bawling and screaming in there. They must have
escaped and got in somehow. I nearly fainted from shock
when . . ."

Mrs. Mac stopped in mid-sentence and stared in
horror as Kay opened the kitchen door and rushed into
the hall calling me. More roars came from the study.
Mrs. Mac was utterly astounded to hear me rush past and
straight out to the zoo. She followed, assuming I was
making a run for it. Kay called her back and spent some
time calming the poor lady and explaining the situation.

When I got to the enclosure I panted up to the keeper who smiled. All was well. Arja had delivered herself of three beautiful little cubs. Now we had to hope she would not reject or savage them.

Wild animals do not automatically accept and feed their offspring. If there is any problem with their environment when they give birth, if they are upset by something, or if there is something crucially wrong with one of their young, the mother animals will often reject one or all of their litter. Sometimes baby cubs disappear completely and we can only assume they have been eaten after they have died.

The keeper and I tentatively peeked at Arja—we knew our presence could disturb her. To our relief she was licking the cubs clean—a very important sign that she had accepted them.

We continued to keep as close a watch on them as possible but with great care because if we stayed too long or bothered her too much we knew Arja might take it out on the cubs. This was in the days before closed-circuit television was freely available, so we had to be content to look in from time to time, staying no more than a few minutes on each occasion. We could not be certain that she was feeding the cubs adequately but she didn't seem to be neglecting them. All we could do between visits was to listen on the loudspeakers; the types of sounds coming from the cage assured us that they were alive and content.

However, as time passed, it gradually became clear that she was neglecting this litter just as she had the first one. The cubs, which had been very small at birth, were not putting on much weight or gaining in strength; in fact they seemed to be growing more listless.

At the end of a week, we got the mother out of the cage in order to weigh the cubs. We found one of them, a male, in fine condition, though slightly underweight for his age. Another, a female, was very weak and sickly, and significantly under-weight. The third one was dead.

Once again there was nothing for it but to take them into the house and hand-rear them. The strong, healthy male I christened Buster and we called his sister Not-So-Good for obvious reasons. As there were only the two of them, and as Not-So-Good needed intensive care and attention, we decided that it would not be necessary to look for a foster mother as we had for the previous tiger cubs, but would bring them up, like the baby lion Sampson, on the bottle. We started them off on glucose and water, and then the vet put them on glucose saline drips as well. Before long they were as happy and as healthy as the first four cubs had been. I became particularly friendly with Buster and I often took him for walks around the grounds, even when he grew quite large.

We had them vaccinated against feline enteritis. Even after this precaution, when eventually they had to be moved into the cage, I made sure that they were kept at all times behind glass. Buster remained very amicable. He would always come right to the front of the cage to greet me. I would stroke him, ruffling up the fur behind his ears, the way you pet any dog or cat, and he'd purr loudly.

Then one day some friends visited the zoo. I took them around and when we approached Buster's enclosure I told them what great pals we were and how tame and affectionate he was. I stepped behind the barrier rail in front of his cage and called him over to me. I suppose I was showing off, impressing my friends with my ability to handle wild creatures. Anyway, I broke an important rule and paid the price. As I stroked Buster I turned my back on him to chat to my friends.

It was a silly mistake. Suddenly I felt a sharp nip on my hand as he closed his teeth neatly on my finger. It was only a playful bite, the sort of bite the cubs were always giving one another, out of affection as they romped and played. If he hadn't been playing he would have bitten my finger right off.

Of course I could have explained all this to my friends but I was so ashamed, so mortified at what they would think about me being treated in this way by my great friend Buster, that I simply slipped my hand into my pocket to hide the blood.

I remember walking across the grounds with my friends, hustling them out really, all the time feeling the blood running down the inside of my leg from my trouser pocket. As soon as they had gone I went to the hospital and had my hand stitched.

Buster lived to the age of fourteen, a fair age for a tiger and Not-So-Good turned out to be a fine animal, despite our initial misgivings.

I am proud to say that we have also been successful in breeding clouded leopards, very rare and beautiful animals from South-East Asia which are high on the list of the endangered species. By the late sixties I had started on what later became my real policy: to concentrate on breeding endangered species.

In 1968 I heard on the animal grapevine that a dealer in the Netherlands had three clouded leopards and that he was on the look-out for wallabies, of which I had a surplus at that particular time. Wallabies are a species of small kangaroo and for some reason, probably because they come from Tasmania which has a climate rather similar to our own, we found that they breed very well in Dublin.

I flew out to Amsterdam where I was met by the

dealer who took me to his home. After a meal and a chat, I went out to examine the leopards which were being kept near his house. They were very tame and I was able to satisfy myself that they were exactly what I wanted: one male and two females, half grown and in very good shape. I arranged to send him ten or twelve wallabies in exchange for the leopards.

The clouded leopards, which had been imported direct from Asia, were probably seven or eight months old and they soon settled down very happily in the zoo. Officially the females were known as Rita and Sita, but I always called Rita "Bad Tail" because she tended to lose the hair around the base of her tail. There is a tendency to choose names for animals which make it easy to identify them quickly—Bad Eye, Scarleg, Limpy and so on. But for the sake of stud book reference, all our animals have official names as well.

Few zoos had then succeeded in breeding clouded leopards and we too had endless trouble in the early stages. In 1970 Sita gave birth to two cubs, reared them almost to maturity when they both mysteriously died. We never found out why. Then Rita gave birth to a single cub but neglected it completely. Although we desperately tried hand-rearing, it died within two weeks. In the early part of 1972 both females bred again and the two sets of cubs died within a few days of birth; Rita, in fact, ate her two cubs, probably because they had died.

Our first thought was that the breeding quarters were not suitable, so we decided to improve their dens. We used glass to make them quieter and then fitted them with a closed-circuit television system, so that we could observe the mothers' behaviour immediately after birth.

Sita gave birth to two more cubs in June 1972. We watched the births on television but within hours the cubs had completely disappeared. We assumed they had died and been eaten by Sita, but we couldn't tell why. Something was upsetting her.

Shortly after Sita lost her third litter, Rita began to lose her coat, mainly around her tail, so I took her away to our hospital quarters. We were not sure whether her skin condition was contagious and we did not want her to pass it on to the others. We also wanted to isolate her completely so that we could take samples of her skin and fur, and do a number of medical tests on her coat. She was kept in a small cage with a box to sleep in. There, in the cramped conditions of the hospital, she suddenly gave birth to two cubs. We were completely taken aback; we hadn't even suspected that she was pregnant. It is usually very hard to tell without a clinical examination whether some of the big cats are pregnant.

This time, to our suprise, she licked the cubs clean and immediately allowed them to start feeding. Since everything seemed to be going so well, we left her where she was in a very small cage in the hospital, and she reared the two youngsters perfectly—no problems at all.

I tried to think of some explanation—what was so good about the hospital? She had reared these cubs in a tiny, uncomfortable cage. The other animals in the hospital at that particular time were a gibbon, a couple of macaws and some Asian otters—all very noisy animals which I would have thought would disturb her. Then I realized—most of them were species from her own part of the world.

In the enclosure she could hear a lot of extraneous noises, particularly around feeding time: the voices of the keepers; the noise of the food barrows being wheeled around; the traps in the other cats' cages being opened; the sounds the other cats made eating; the noises made by the keepers when cleaning out the cages; and all the time of course, the noise created by the public, especially the children, outside the enclosure.

In the hospital, which was tucked away in a very quiet corner of the zoo never visited by the public, she could hear no human noises at all—only the gibbon, the otters and the macaws.

When Sita became pregnant again, I moved her up to the hospital wing where she had a litter of two healthy cubs which she proceeded to rear without mishap.

We had hit on the answer by sheer chance. Since then we have been breeding these very attractive and extremely valuable animals regularly and successfully, and I like to think that we are improving the chances of survival for this very rare breed.

But apart from the actual joy of managing to breed the clouded leopard they were also important to the zoo —not only as an attraction but as animals to exchange for equally interesting and rare species. We made arrangements with a zoo in Finland to exchange a pair of clouded leopards for a pair of snow leopards. Unfortunately it turned out that Finland could only part with a female snow leopard. With rare creatures such as these a stud book is kept in one place to record where each of a species is kept and precisely what animals are available. My contacts in Finland held the stud book for snow leopards and they helped me track down a suitable male.

Cincinnati Zoo in the United States have one and I am now making arrangements with them to have this snow leopard on what we call a breeding loan. If I can successfully breed from my female and their male in the Dublin Zoo, they will have first option on half of any litter produced. This is now common and a very satisfactory arrangement. I must also be prepared to return their snow leopard if Cincinnati urgently require a male.

It had always been my ambition to have a pair of gorillas

in the Dublin Zoo but it wasn't easy to fulfil because they are extremely scarce and very expensive—around £5,000 each at least—and you really need a pair. It is not fair to keep one gorilla on its own in captivity. They are the largest of the apes. Two types exist: the Lowland gorilla of the equatorial forests of West Africa and the Mountain gorilla from Eastern Zaire and South-west Uganda which are extremely rare.

An animal dealer in England telephoned me one day with good news.

"Still on the look-out for gorillas, Terry?" she asked. "Because if you are, I think I've found a couple for you." And she went on to tell me about two gorillas which had been ordered for a zoo in England: the deal had fallen through and the import licence had run out so that these gorillas, which were in quarantine in Austria, were going at a bargain price. If I was quick about it, I could probably get the pair for less than the going rate for a single specimen.

I put it to the Council, got immediate agreement and made a deal. They were young animals, both in the thirty to forty pound range; again, this was important because unless they are roughly the same weight, one will dominate the other. All seemed set fair, but when the plane arrived there was only one gorilla on board: a fine male specimen weighing thirty-nine pounds, called Gusto. The female died in Austria.

I now had one male gorilla and desperately needed a companion for him. Gusto had come from a Viennese dealer who now promised to find a replacement for the female, from the Cameroons in West Africa. He knew I wanted an animal weighing about thirty pounds. When the replacement arrived, in November 1972, she weighed only eleven pounds and was packed—that's the only word you could use—in a box rather like a large biscuit tin. She had originally been called Gabrielle, we changed her name to Yinka.

She was about three or four months old and still suckling. Yinka had come by air from the Cameroons via France to Cork airport and finally up to Dublin. The journey had nearly killed her. In fact none of us thought she would survive. There was no question of putting her in the enclosure with Gusto; she was clearly going to need all the care and attention we could give her.

Our graphic artist, Jill Breivick who designed labels for cages and all the signs and posters in the zoo, was exceptionally good with animals. I installed Yinka in a room in the office section of the house, and Jill took on Yinka as well as her normal duties, but Yinka was to be her priority. Gorillas are extraordinarily like humans and what this animal principally needed was mothering. I told Jill this and explained to her that the gorilla was very much like a human baby and would need just as much attention.

Jill reacted marvellously. She was with Yinka every day from nine o'clock in the morning until six or seven in the evening, nursing her on her lap like a baby: playing with her, feeding her from a bottle and with little morsels of solid food, and carrying her around the house in her arms. Within a few days the pair of them were inseparable. At the same time, Jill kept a complete daily record of every scrap of food the baby gorilla ate, noting down how she reacted to the various diets we tried out, and logging her weight, temperature, behaviour and responses. It's a fantastic document, an hour-by-hour account of the animal's recovery, with enough detail to enable us to see which treatments were working, which were not, and precisely what effect every variation of diet had upon the animal.

Initially Yinka continued to lose weight, sometimes

more than half a pound a day, but we soon got the right diet: (a mixture of lactol, milk and banana, mashed up with a little meat for protein and the whole lot put through a liquidizer) and Yinka began to put on weight rapidly. Before long Jill was able to take her out. Yinka seemed very happy and contented.

The evenings were a problem, though. As soon as Jill went home, Yinka would immediately start to fret and cry because she was so dependent upon her. Devoted as she was to Yinka, we could not ask Jill to stay with the gorilla all evening as well as all day.

I don't know who hit on the idea of television, but one day it was suggested to me that if we were to put a colour television set in the room with Yinka, all the colour and light and movement might give her the impression that she wasn't really alone. It worked like a charm. The television was turned on while Jill was with her and they watched it together. Yinka began to associate the television with Jill and soon she hardly even noticed Jill's absence as long as the television was on. She was absolutely fascinated and would stare at it hour after hour. She had her preferences, of course. Westerns were her number one favourite but any programme with plenty of action and noise went down well. She was also very fond of musical shows but not at all keen on the news or current affairs programmes. She continued to watch them, like a small child, in the hope that something more interesting would come along soon.

The idea of bringing up a baby gorilla with the help of a colour television set held an immediate appeal for the newspapers and stories about Yinka soon went out around the world. I also did several interviews for both radio and television.

I remember one interview, live on the telephone from my office, for Canadian radio. The one thing that seemed to interest the interviewer was Yinka's reaction to blue movies. I was happy to be able to assure him smugly that this was Ireland where blue movies are never shown on the television and Yinka was totally uncorrupted.

When the programmes finished around midnight, either Martin Reid or I would go in and give her her supper and like any well brought up human child, she seemed to sense that the evening's entertainment was now over and it was time to go to bed. She was usually only just beginning to wake up when Jill arrived the next morning.

Finally we got Yinka to the stage where she was able to look after herself. We decided to try her in the cage with Gusto but the difference in weight and size was really far too great. By now Gusto weighed over fifty pounds and Yinka only twenty-five or thirty. He was very rough with her in a playful way and she was clearly terrified out of her wits. She also pined constantly for Jill. We had to separate the gorillas and only allow them together very occasionally and under close surveillance. Yinka was a quiet, delicate, nervous little animal. If I had been taking any bets on their chances of survival I would certainly have put all my money on Gusto but he caught virus pneumonia in 1975 and died very suddenly, despite all our efforts to save him.

The problem now was to get another companion for Yinka. By this time gorillas were fetching up to £7,000 on the open market. Fortunately zoos were working in much closer collaboration with one another, and trading directly with each other. I discovered from the gorilla studbook that Nuremberg Zoo had a young gorilla for sale which was about the right size and weight. Gori, as he was called, weighed fifty pounds and by now Yinka weighed about the same, if not a little more. I travelled to Germany to inspect him and found him to be in perfect shape.

I was concerned about how he would fare on the journey from Germany to Ireland. As usual, Aer Lingus, the Irish airline, were very helpful and accommodating. Ideally, I wanted him to travel in the passenger section where the stewardesses would keep an eye on him and where it was heated, but this was out of the question. He had to travel in the forward luggage compartment which can be dangerously cold. The airline tried to arrange a special flight plan so that they could maintain a low altitude and a higher temperature inside the plane.

Gori arrived safely, wrapped in blankets and we introduced him to Yinka soon afterwards. They got along famously. Yinka was slightly larger, and on her own territory, so she took control.

So far there is no sign of them breeding but you must remember that they are both, relatively speaking, still in their early teens. There is plenty of time yet.

Yinka was successfully reared with help of television— other babies required less sophisticated mother substitutes.

Soon after a baby Colobus monkey was born its mother caught a serious cold which developed into pneumonia. Just twenty-eight hours after the baby was born, the mother died.

The Colobus are rare monkeys and we had been thrilled when they bred. Now we were very concerned that the baby would die. Like most baby monkeys the young Colobus would normally cling to its mother by closing its tiny hands tightly over her fur. This baby transferred to its father, who seemed quite happy to accept it and carry it around, but obviously was no mother substitute. We had no alternative but to remove the baby. Although the baby could now be fed it appeared to be terribly upset, as was its father.

We hoped we could solve the baby's problem by taking the same action as we had when faced with a similar predicament some time before. We got a towel.

It had worked for the Mangabay and it worked for the Colobus. We used a black and white striped towel to match the monkey's natural colouring, and hung it on his cage. He clung to it constantly and was happy and content.

It is wonderful when things turn out well like that but there are also times when terrible mistakes occur. One of my earliest and most ridiculous errors caused the death of another baby who needed to cling on to a parent.

When a pair of marmosets produced a delightful little baby we decided it would be wise, as is often done, to remove the father. We had watched them and it appeared that one parent was constantly trying to snatch the baby from the other. I assumed that the animal the baby was clinging to most of the time was the mother so I removed the other to end the conflict.

It was an awful blunder on my part. Baby marmosets, I found out later, cling to their fathers most of the time. When feeding time comes around the female takes the baby. What we had thought was conflict over the baby was in fact a normal process. I removed not the father but the mother from the cage. The next day the baby marmoset was dead—I had starved it quite inadvertently.

I was certainly right to remove the father in the case of another baby: the first Black rhino ever born of parents reared in captivity, though that episode nearly ended in tragedy, too.

There are five species of rhinoceros in the world today: two in Africa—the Black and White rhinoceros; which are actually about the same shade of grey; the white in the case of the latter refers to its wide mouth and the word white is a corruption of "wide" in an African dialect. The Black rhino which has a prehensile mouth is merely called "black" to underline the contrast. There are three in Asia—the Great Indian rhinoceros, found in Bengal, Assam and Eastern Nepal, and also the extremely rare Javan and Sumatran varieties. All the species are hunted, owing to the widely spread belief that the horn, when powdered down, makes a powerful aphrodisiac.

In May 1962 I bought a young female Black rhino called Laura from Rotterdam Zoo where she had been born and reared. The following year I managed to find a mate for her, Ronald, a young male black which had been born and reared in Bristol Zoo. In the case of both Laura and Ronald, one or other of their parents had come from the wild; the same thing applied to all black rhinos born in zoos until then. No zoo had succeeded in breeding from a pair both of whom were born and reared in captivity. I could see no reason why it should be impossible and was certainly going to try.

To my delight Ronald and Laura proved to be perfectly compatible and in 1969 Laura became pregnant. As this was, in zoological circles, an historic event, elaborate precautions were taken. Laura was transferred to a special maternity stall which I had built for her. This was at the rear of the Rhino House, out of reach of the public, and only her keepers were allowed near her. During the last few weeks of the pregnancy a careful watch was maintained night and day by means of a closed-circuit television camera strategically placed in a position which gave a view of almost the whole stall, and relayed a picture to a monitor screen in the corner of the public area of the Rhino House. There it could be viewed at night without disturbing the animals. The night security guards were instructed to keep an hourly check on this monitor screen.

On Wednesday, July 9, my telephone rang at 1:45 A.M. It was one of the security guards. "Mr. Murphy," he said. "I'm sorry to disturb you at this hour of the night, but I think it has started happening."

In a few minutes I was down in the Rhino House with my face glued to the monitor screen. There were no complications and within an hour the young rhino, a male, was standing up and managing to walk, unsteadily, after his mother. He was about two feet long and about a foot and a half high. Two round patches on the top of his nose were the only indication of his future horns. I would dearly like to have gone around to the maternity stall to take a closer look at him in the flesh but I resisted the temptation in case it upset Laura.

After watching them for half an hour or so on the screen I went back to bed because everything seemed in order, though I did ask the security man to continue his hourly checks on the monitor, just in case.

At 5:30 A.M., the telephone rang again. "I'm terribly sorry to disturb you again, Mr. M." he said, "but the baby rhino is after disappearing. I can't see sight nor sign of him anywhere on the screen."

I jumped out of bed again, threw on some clothes and dashed across to the Rhino House to find Laura in a state of extreme agitation and the father, Ronald, in an uncharacteristically aggressive mood. When I entered the service passage I found that the baby had somehow squeezed through the bars of the maternity stall and had wandered down the passage way towards his father's stall. Ronald, who didn't recognize the little creature as his own offspring, was attempting to savage him through the bars, stabbing at the defenceless baby with his ferocious horns. I arrived just in time because the young rhino was totally unaware of any danger and completely without fear.

I snatched him up in my arms—and he was quite an armful—avoiding a few thrusts from Ronald's horns but as I approached the maternity stall and Laura saw me with her baby in my arms, she turned as aggressive as Ronald and began to charge the bars. It was clearly going to be impossible to open the gate because she had made up her mind that it was I who had stolen her baby. On the other hand, if I tried to push the baby back through the bars, this could take several minutes during which there was always the chance that she would injure him in trying to get at me. I made a few attempts to slip the baby rhino through smartly, but Laura rushed the bars each time and knocked both me and the baby over. Finally the security man managed to distract her attention for long enough to enable me to squeeze the baby through the bars all in one piece. Laura immediately calmed down and, whimpering with delight, nuzzled up to the baby which immediately started to feed.

To prevent any recurrence of the incident we built a temporary barricade against the bars with bales of straw. So the baby, a unique animal in his way, survived only as a result of a combination of closed-circuit television technology and the watchfulness of an observant security man. There is no doubt at all that if I had not arrived when I did, Ronald would have killed his son.

A local newspaper co-operated with us in running a competition to find a name for our very special new baby. Thousands of children took part and the name finally chosen was Ringo.

Ringo grew up to be a strong, healthy Black rhino.

Tiger cub and foster-mother—Flossie the collie and one of the babies she helped us rear.

Sampson the lion cub
above whom we
hand-reared. He remained
a playmate of mine until
he was almost too big to
handle *left*.

opposite Toots was the
other foster-mother—each
collie cared for two cubs
plus their own pups—who
joined us in our home when
these tiger cubs were born.

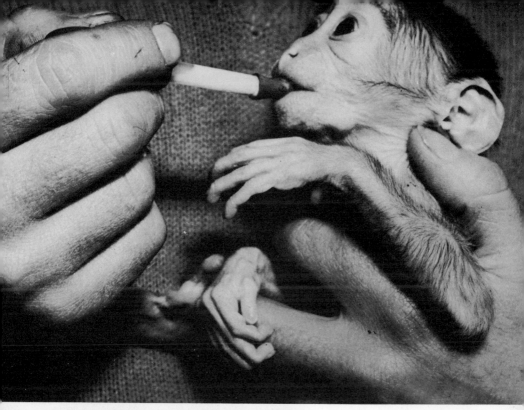

This baby Mangabay monkey was fed by me *above* but a piece of cloth became his real mother substitute *opposite*.

left Pooh-bah is formally introduced to a pair of new-born lion cubs.

above Bashful the giraffe with her baby Happy.

right The new giraffe enclosure has no visible barriers but a dike separates it from the public path.

opposite Komali soon after she arrived from Sri Lanka.

Sarah and Komali became
the best of friends.

right Komali occasionally
performed for visitors in
the "circus" ring beside
the old elephant enclosure

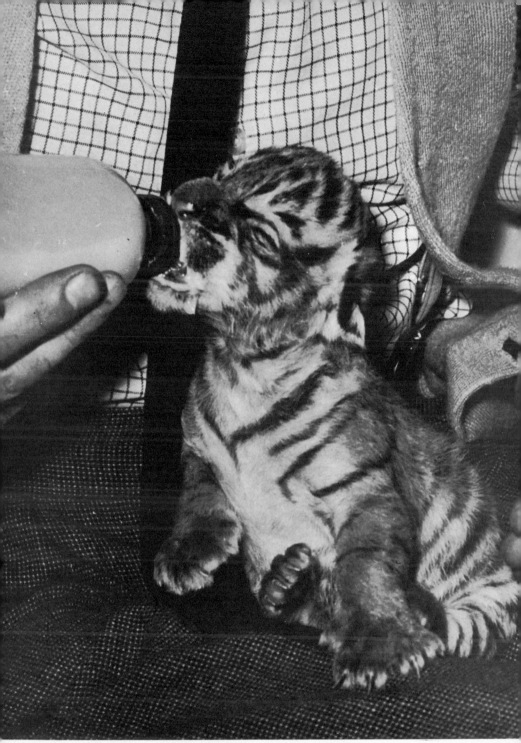

The second litter of tiger cubs to be reared in our home had no foster-mothers but were fed on the bottle—here I was feeding Buster.

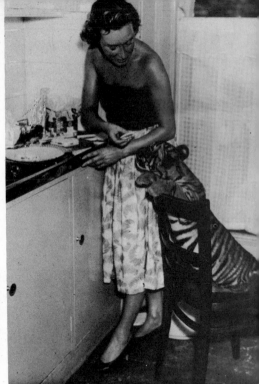

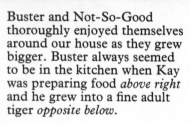

Buster and Not-So-Good
thoroughly enjoyed themselves
around our house as they grew
bigger. Buster always seemed
to be in the kitchen when Kay
was preparing food *above right*
and he grew into a fine adult
tiger *opposite below*.

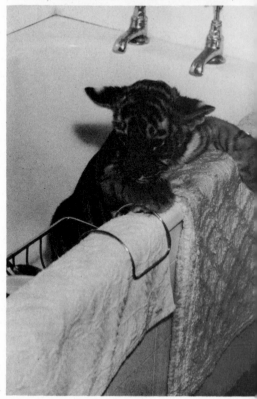

above Gori the male gorilla chews on a ball.

left Yinka, Gori's mate.

opposite Rita, a splendid clouded leopard, gave birth to these two delightful cubs and gave us the distinction of being one of the few zoos to breed these cats.

overleaf Yinka (left) and Gori have a slight disagreement.

above I had to remove this Colobus monkey and hand-rear it after
its mother died.

left Yinka was frail and unwell when she arrived in the zoo but
soon recovered with the help of Jill Breivick who cared for her.

Laura the rhinoceros with her son Ringo.

Troubles And Tranquillizers

I HAVE TO ADMIT to a certain sneaking admiration for the fox. The fox is one of the only wild animals that has come to terms with civilization, and has never allowed it to beat him. There are wild foxes in Dublin suburbs, in obvious areas like the Phoenix Park but also in St. Stephen's Green and Herbert Park which are right in the heart of the city. They can live on derelect sites by hunting anything that is available: birds, mice, and even snails: and by scavenging in dustbins.

But much as I admire them for their tenacity, in the zoo we are always extremely apprehensive when we know they are around, and they are around a great deal. In fact they probably cause us more problems than any other species—including *homo sapiens.*

Like most other animals, foxes have their own territories which completely disregard man-made boundaries. They simply ignore fences as if they do not exist and continue to use the whole of an area as their territory by clambering over the fences, if possible, or by scraping under them.

Unlike other animals, foxes do not appear to follow a regular hunting pattern. They double back and forth, using different parts of their range on different nights, in what seems to us to be a completely haphazard way. It so happened that the ranges of a number of foxes which lived in the Phoenix Park included sections of the Zoological Gardens. Obviously an area containing many small animals and plump, delicious birds is extremely tempting to a fox. We have tried constantly to ensure that our animals are well protected by erecting "fox-proof" fencing but inevitably some of them managed to break through. One fox kept coming in for a long time, and always took his prey from our Pets Corner, where we kept a number of small animals which appealed to children: rabbits, ducklings, fawns, kittens, sometimes a lamb—all easy prey for a hungry fox.

Eventually we had to set up Council of War. For many nights we sat up—myself, Tom, the zoo's electrician, Martin, and a few keepers—to try to spot him, and work out how and where he was getting in. One night, as we began our vigil it started to snow lightly.

"Now's our chance," Martin said. "If he comes tonight, he's bound to leave footprints in the snow. So it's only a question of following them and then we'll know how he gets in."

Martin and the keepers were watching from the restaurant and I was in the house. Martin was absolutely right about the snow. Glancing out after three hours or so, I saw fresh tracks in front of the house. I telephoned the restaurant to say the fox was on the prowl.

The tracks were easy enough to follow and they led us right across the gardens to an aviary, where they suddenly disappeared. I opened up the aviary, but there was no sign of any carnage or the fox.

I was just about to give the whole thing up as a bad

job, when I noticed that the tracks continued on the far side of the aviary. The fox had obviously realized that he was being tracked and had jumped up on to the aviary roof. A brilliant feat, as it was over eight feet high. He had crossed it, in an effort to give us the slip. They are not exaggerating when they say "cute as a fox." We didn't find him that night. By the time we had picked up the tracks again the snow had almost stopped, and we soon lost him again.

We immediately changed direction and followed the tracks back to discover how our bushy-tailed predator had entered the zoo. Again, his actions had shown great intelligence. He had used a bush in order to get high enough to jump over the railings and the "fox-proof" wire mesh. We cut down the bush and increased the height of the railings which solved the problem.

On one night alone, another fox killed five birds. We knew that two geese were missing, and we knew that he'd taken them, but what does a fox do with birds as large as geese? He could not possibly have eaten them all. A goose is heavier than a fox and it's as much as one fox can do to haul away the carcass of a single goose. Also they're lone hunters; they never go in packs.

Putting myself in his position, I tried to imagine what I would do if I were a fox and had succeeded in killing two geese and three ducks. It seemed to me that the most sensible thing to do would be to bury four of them, and come back for them later. I'd then carry away the fifth.

Acting on this supposition, Martin and I examined the grounds for signs of fresh digging, and found some recently upturned soil in a rose bed just outside the window of the house. We dug there and uncovered the carcass of one duck. We then found the remains of a goose in my garage. We reckoned that he would eventually return to the vicinity of the house.

I sat up night after night, determined to catch this cheeky thief. I would sit by my bedroom window looking out over the areas by the house, ready to shoot him from the window if necessary. We had installed powerful spotlights to illuminate the grounds. My weapon was an ancient shot gun. As I sat there for the first couple of nights I knew this was going to be a battle of nerves. I imagined the fox approaching the zoo and not daring to enter the brightly lit area where previously, under the cover of darkness, he had stored his prey or enjoyed a satisfying meal. But I knew that if I kept my patience long enough, his hunger would lead him to take risks, and sure enough it did.

One night I spotted him moving quickly towards the main section of the zoo. I was so anxious and keyed-up my finger slipped while cocking the gun and I jumped out of my seat in terror as it went off, spraying shot on the floor. Kay woke up screaming, only to see me dashing out of the bedroom in hot pursuit of the fox. But I knew when I got outside that I had lost him. However my shock at hearing the shot gun blast was, I knew, nothing compared to the fox's. I was convinced he would remain in the zoo for the rest of the night, too scared to venture back near the house. I returned inside to find Kay looking in horror at the holes I had made in our bedroom carpet.

Early next morning I called on Martin, who also lives on the premises, and we set off to find the fox. He ran out from a bush several hundred yards in front of us and as Martin and I ran towards him we saw him jump on to a wall near the polar bear enclosure.

This attractive home for the bears contained a construction of granite rocks, covered in ivy, about thirty feet high, which formed a background for the animals, with an area of flat concrete in front, separated from the public by a deep ditch filled with water.

It was into this ivy that the cornered fox now darted. As we approached the enclosure in the dim grey light of dawn, we saw him teetering on the top of the granite rocks. He missed his foothold and fell down into the enclosure. One of the bears sprang up, caught the fox and killed him before he had time to hit the water. There was not even a scream. It was all over in a split second.

The polar bear is the one animal that I would not like to have loose in the zoo grounds. An elephant is dangerous enough, or a lion, but they're child's play to deal with, compared with polar bears. If either of the bears escaped, which is highly unlikely, I wouldn't even try to use a tranquillizer gun. The only solution would be to shoot it if we couldn't get it back inside its enclosure. They are terribly dangerous and much bigger than they seem to be. They are also among the only animals that will attack without any provocation. In their enclosure they appear to be peaceful, lumbering creatures but they are surprisingly fast. Even in their own environment in the Arctic, they have been known to chase men over considerable distances and without any apparent provocation.

Around this time, we had a lot of trouble with another predator—this time an otter. They are beautiful creatures and very graceful in water. This particular otter killed a magnificent white swan and two of our rare and beautiful black swans. He had to be stopped but I did not, under any circumstances, want to kill him. Otters are a threatened species.

We could tell from his tracks that he was an unusually big specimen and that he was coming into the zoo through a culvert. The zoo's electrician devised a clever trap and we caught him there, in the culvert. I had no suitable home for him so he was sent to another zoo.

Later, we built an otter enclosure with a glass-fronted pool for them to swim in, so that the public could watch their antics under water. I had no problem finding otters. One was found in County Kildare by a farmer and another came from a bank. The manager had found it one morning and when I arrived to collect it, he was feeding the young otter from a tin of salmon. They are beautifully graceful and playful animals, especially in the water and they became a big attraction at the zoo.

Nevertheless one of them managed to escape and headed down to the lake where he led us a merry dance. Sammy, as we called him, was on the loose for about a week. We could follow his progress up and down the lake by the streams of bubbles that issued from his nostrils whenever he came up to breathe, but he paid no attention at all to the many traps we set for him. One day, when we caught him peeping out at us from behind a bush where he was enjoying the remains of a meal, we knew we had him. The keeper with me fetched the tranquillizer gun and knocked him out with that.

When he recovered consciousness, he was back in the otter enclosure with his mate.

Tranquillizer or capture guns have only been developed to the point where they are really useful in zoos in relatively recent years. They are an enormous asset, especially in helping us to capture escaped animals without endangering the lives of keepers and without having to resort to rifles.

The capture gun used in zoos is a largish pistol, similar to an air gun, which fires the missile by compressed air. The missile, is, in effect, no more than a hypodermic syringe; but a syringe with a difference. The needle has a flange on it which holds it in place in case the animal tries to shake it loose, and the main body of the syringe has a small charge of explosive behind the drug which is set off by the impact of the needle against the animal. The resultant explosion, in the body of the syringe, drives the piston down and forces the tranquillizer through the needle into the animal.

One drug we use is a muscle relaxant and the dose has to be very carefully calculated according to the species and weight of the animal. If you administer an underdose, there is always the danger that the animal will regain full control of its limbs too soon. On the other hand, an overdose could cause the muscles of the heart to relax and stop beating, and the animal could die of heart failure. The doses have been carefully charted and accidents are rare, though they still happen.

The gun is not only used when an animal escapes. We need to tranquillize a large animal in order to give it a medical examination or treatment. Obviously for creatures such as giraffes, it is both unpleasant and dangerous for them to be manoeuvred into a cage so that an injection can be administered. Now we can fire the syringe into the animal while it remains in its own enclosure.

On one occasion, I was down in Rosslare playing golf when I got an urgent message to return to the zoo. I knew something was going to go wrong that day, because I had sliced my first drive wildly into the golf club car park, smashing the headlamp of a new car; it would have to be a new car wouldn't it? Leaving my card under the windscreen wiper, I went back to my game, only to be accosted as I approached the second tee, by one of those small red-haired boys who abound in all Irish golf clubs, ready to do anything from help in the restaurant, to act as caddy or advise you on your play.

"Mr. Murphy," he shouted. "A desperate emergency in the Dublin Zoo. All the monkeys is after escaping and if you don't get back immediately, they're going to bring in the police and shoot them all."

I suspected that this was the Irish talent for melodrama expressing itself at an early age; it was impossible that all the monkeys in the zoo could have escaped simultaneously, and I could not believe that the police would be quite so precipitate. Normally they trusted us to get things under control in our own time and in our own way. So before jumping into the car and speeding off to Dublin, I rang Martin. Things were not nearly as bad as the boy had indicated, but the situation was serious. Three chimpanzees had escaped including one very special animal, Cholmondeley, who was on loan from Gerald Durrell's Jersey zoo. The zoo had been full of visitors and the chimps were big enough to do a great deal of damage. Martin had cleared the grounds without mishap, and two of the chimps had been recaptured. But Cholmondeley was still at large. The police were on hand in case he should get clear of the grounds but Martin assured me that this was unlikely.

"We have the capture gun ready," Martin said.

"You'd better telephone Gerald Durrell," I suggested, "and check on the dosage to use."

Martin said he'd do that immediately and I rushed to my car and headed home. It was a hundred mile drive to Dublin. By the time I arrived, about an hour later, Cholmondeley was dying from an overdose of the tranquillizer drug. I was told the whole, tragic story.

The chimp had run into one of the public toilets near the entrance to the zoo. He was hit by a tranquillizer dart just before he went in, but it didn't appear to be working. The next thing that Martin, the keepers and the police witnessed was Cholmondeley emerging on to the roof of the toilets. He was then in a position, right at the edge of the zoo, from which he could easily escape to the outside world. Partly in panic at this prospect—and it must be remembered that fully-grown male chimpanzees can be extremely dangerous—and partly as a result of over-caution, a second dart was fired and hit him. He received far more of the tranquillizer drug than Jersey Zoo had advised. I blamed no one, it had been an error on the side of safety, but a tragedy just the same.

To use an underdose accidentally is perhaps even more dangerous, as I discovered with nearly disastrous results.

In this instance we were dealing with a tigress who was due to have cubs. She had gone well over the gestation period and warranted a visit from the vet. We put her under, or so we thought, with precisely the right amount of muscle relaxant for a tigress of her size.

The vet was perfectly satisfied that she was adequately sedated and proceeded with his examination. He emerged from the cage and we discussed his diagnosis with the keeper. The vet was not completely sure that he found the cause of the delay in giving birth and asked the keeper to unlock the cage again so he could make a further examination.

I had a premonition. I was nervous that the drug could have worn off—even though she was lying rigidly on the floor. We lifted the cage door and I leaned over, very cautiously. I touched the animal gently while the door of the cage was still open. She jumped up instantly and turned to face us, snarling savagely. We had to slam the door down with immense speed. The tigress was fully awake and in complete possession of all her faculties.

What had happened? Maybe the full dose had not gone in; maybe this tigress was resistant, as some humans are, to even quite large quantities of drugs; or maybe the drug was stale or defective.

The interesting thing was that throughout this entire period the tigress had lain perfectly still. My own view is that the drug had taken effect and then gradually worn off. The tigress had realized she was debilitated, and she was not going to stagger to her feet in a dazed condition. She had remained still until the strength had sufficiently returned to her limbs. If the vet had gone in, he would not have stood a chance with an angry tigress in that confined space.

Modern drugs and the tranquillizer gun have made things a lot easier for people who work with animals. But like all modern inventions, they have their limitations and have to be used with extreme caution.

I cannot even look at a capture gun without remembering one highly dramatic incident. The whole affair was humourously christened by one of the local newspapers —though it wasn't in the least funny at the time—"High Noon at Dublin Zoo." Ironically, it involved the chimpanzee we had acquired to replace the ill-fated Cholmondeley.

His name suited him well. Congola was a splendid specimen—big, muscular and arrogant, with massive arms and powerful thighs. He was not an animal to tamper with and as popular as he was with the chimpanzee colony, none of the human beings around the zoo wanted any personal contact with Congola, and Frank, his keeper, was no exception.

Looking around one day, as he was cleaning the night quarters of the chimps' enclosure, he saw one, big chimp's foot stepping into the service passage from the outer enclosure: Congola had somehow managed to open a door. Frank was determined he wouldn't find a single, defenceless keeper! He charged out of the chimps' house and locked the main door securely behind him. He then had to raise the alarm.

He found the nearest two-way radio and announced to the zoo staff: "Congola is out of his enclosure but is locked inside the Chimpanzee House."

I got on the radio immediately and asked the staff to begin calmly asking any visitors in the vicinity of the chimps' enclosure to move back. Frank went off to fetch the travelling cage in which Congola had arrived at the zoo, and I loaded a capture gun—just in case. The plan was simple: we would open one door of the chimps' enclosure, place the cage at that door and then coax Congola into it with his favourite food.

Congola was already making quite sure that plan was not going to be executed. As I walked towards my car with the capture gun, Martin's voice came over the radio. Congola was on the roof of the night quarters—he had forced open a skylight. The emergency alarm rang through the zoo and every member of staff went into action.

Martin and several other men got into a van and drove over towards the enclosure. Martin took the sensible precaution of carrying a loaded rifle. The visitors were either locked into buildings, or, if they were near an exit, quickly escorted outside. The gates were shut and we all held our breath in anticipation of Congola's next move.

As I drove over to the enclosure I spotted him and gave Martin and the others his location over the radio. In such situations our basic plan of action is usually the same. We cut off all routes except one so the animal does not feel completely cornered and also so that the animal's escape route is in the direction we want him to go.

I stopped my car several yards from Congola. He proceeded to behave just as most chimps do when they feel excited. He beat his chest, jumping back and forth. Then he stopped for a moment and took a long, meaningful look at my car. Suddenly he charged and bounced off the wing of the car. I backed up for some distance and stepped out, taking the capture gun with me. Martin moved up behind me on foot, armed with the rifle. Apart from a few strategically placed keepers the zoo was deserted and silent. My heart was pounding as I began to stalk towards Congola. He stood facing me, his hands drooping limply by his sides.

I hoped that he would turn and run from me, so using the escape route we had left open which would lead him back towards his enclosure. But Congola held his ground and I stopped moving when I'd got as close as I dared. He pulled a threatening face, grimacing at me and baring his teeth. Then he jumped again, letting out a terrifying scream. He was trying to scare me into moving back. I, too, stood my ground.

Congola decide to take action. He braced himself then charged. I was so close and so frightened, I merely froze on the spot as this huge chimp pounded up to me and sent me flying with his powerful shoulder.

I jumped to my feet, clutching the capture gun, and turned to face him once more. We were now standing on an open expanse of grass in front of the restaurant. Martin and the others slowly changed position, keeping their eyes fixed on Congola. It was a nasty situation. I had to move to within fifteen feet of him to be sure of getting in an accurate shot. I knew if I fired and missed the explosion would panic him and all would be lost.

He was becoming increasingly agitated and, as he

peered around, the restaurant caught his eye. Scores of visitors who had been locked inside were crowding against the plate glass window determined not to miss a second of this dramatic incident.

Congola looked long and hard at the faces—all staring at him. In his fury he charged at the restaurant and as people fell back in terror he crashed against the glass feet first. It smashed.

Martin aimed the rifle but Congola didn't try to enter the restaurant. He was shaken and injured—the shattered pane had cut his foot. He turned away, back towards me, and lay down on the grass, crying in pain. I felt an almost uncontrollable impulse to go over and comfort him, but I knew deep down just how dangerous a mood he was in.

He got up and started to move off. I followed him circumspectly, gratefully aware of Martin in the background with the rifle. Every time Congola stopped, I stopped too, trying to edge nearer all the time. He was getting far too close to the main gates of the zoo for comfort. If he got out of the gardens altogether and into the Phoenix Park proper, I knew we would certainly have to kill him.

I had only one dart in the gun, so I could not afford to miss.

The moment of truth arrived. It was now or never. I took careful aim and fired—I hit him in the thigh, exactly where I wanted to. I did not wait to see the drug take effect on him; I took to my heels and ran. Martin told me later that he had chased me for about fifteen yards, screaming and yelling, and had then sat heavily down on the grass and pulled the dart out. This interruption, of which I wasn't even aware, gave me a head start.

When he had removed the dart, he stumbled to his

203

feet and stared after me again. By now the drug was beginning to take effect and after a few yards he sat down again, looking very dazed, then suddenly toppled over and passed out. By this time I was over the hill, far too exhausted to take any further interest in the proceedings. The others carried him back to his cage, locked him up securely and within seven hours he was up and about again, as lively as ever.

My own adrenalin, which had been working over-time, carried me through the rest of the day. But that evening when I was attending a dinner party, my host suddenly remarked that I was looking a little pale.

"You'd probably be looking a little off colour your-self if you'd been chased across the Zoological Gardens by a chimpanzee nearly as tall as yourself and quite a few pounds heavier," I replied.

By now the incident had become a joke, and I must say it made a very good after-dinner story. However, I soon stopped laughing. Later that evening I collapsed with a heart attack.

It's not a sedentary occupation, running a zoo . . .

There was a distinct cooling of our relationship after this incident, mainly on Congola's side. Soon after it happened, we moved him back to the main enclosure among the other chimps. For a while he sat sullenly on top of his pole, completely ignoring me. He knew that I was the one who had fired the dart which brought him down, and was not about to forgive and forget. He had always been a "tough guy" and I do not think he much liked being rendered helpless by a little dart.

It seems he made the mental connection between the gun, the dart and me, though to the best of my know-ledge he'd never seen a dart gun, or any other kind of a gun, in his life before. Some time later I was walking through the grounds and as I approached his enclosure I picked up a stick to test his reactions. His mind must have made the connection instantly; he climbed down from his pole and rushed to hide in his den, not re-appearing for several hours.

I still have to be very wary whenever I go anywhere near the enclosure because he's quite likely to dance around excitedly and then pick up a handful of stones and start throwing them at me. He's a great shot with a stone—deadly accurate. Even when I approach in my car, I'm quite likely to get a broadside. He knows my car and he knows the staff cars and we all get the same kind of treatment. But he has never thrown a single stone at the miniature road train that carries children right past his enclosure.

A Collection
Of Cats

LIONS WERE FIRST exhibited in the Dublin Zoo in
1833. Owing to financial difficulties they were
sold, along with most of the carnivores, in 1847;
this was the period in the immediate wake of the Great
Famine when food and money were still in short supply
throughout the country. The absence of lions brought a
great deal of criticism; whatever other species might be
missing, visitors always expected to see lions in a zoo,
and they still do.

Throughout history the lion has been regarded as
"King of the Beasts" despite the fact that tigers are both
larger and more handsome. A curious affinity seems to
have existed between man and the lion, an animal which
is everywhere regarded as the very epitome of strength
and savage nobility. The very fact that the lion is used as
a trade mark for companies as varied as banks, motor-car
manufacturers, film makers and breweries all over the
world is a proof of the special position this species
occupies in mankind's view of the animal world.

In response to public demand the Council, in 1855,

secured a government grant of £285, then a very con-siderable sum, to buy a pair of lions. In 1857 Natal and Natalie, as they were called, produced the first lion cubs to be born in Dublin and laid the foundation of the breeding stock for which the Dublin Zoo soon became internationally renowned.

Natalie died while nursing her third litter, but one of these, a splendid lioness called Old Girl, gave birth to what was then a record total of fifty-five cubs in thrity-three litters. Two of these litters were sired by her father, Natal, and the other eleven by Old Charlie, a son of Natal and Anonyma, a lioness purchased shortly after Natalie's death.

Old Girl lived for sixteen years and went on pro-ducing cubs until a few years before her death. During the six weeks before she died she was extremely ill and very feeble; she was suffering from chronic arthritis. In those days, hygiene in the zoo was rather poor and it was not uncommon, according to the records, to see rats gnawing at the remains of the bones left in the cages after the lions had eaten. As Old Girl was able to move only with the greatest of difficulty, and was quite in-capable of chasing the rats away, they grew bolder and finally began to nibble at her paws. In an effort to rid her of this torment, the keeper tried putting a small terrier dog into the cage with her. If she had been stronger, there is no doubt that she would quickly have killed and eaten him. The terrier kept his distance and all Old Girl was capable of doing was to growl ineffectually. After a few days, when the terrier had killed several rats in the cage and banished all the others, Old Girl seemed to realize what he was doing and accepted him, eventually encouraging the dog to come to her. She would gently fold her paws around him in the most affectionate manner. For the following few weeks, until she died, the terrier always slept between her paws.

To reduce the possibility of congenital defects developing through excessive in-breeding, new blood was introduced from time to time. One new arrival, Selim Bey, was presented to the Society by Sir Geoffrey Archer, Governor of Uganda. Before his death from enteritis in 1927 Selim Bey served one lioness, Deirdre, who produced two cubs. Legend has it that one of these, Cairbre, was the original Metro-Goldwyn-Meyer lion. Cairbre sired a total of seventy-two cubs, and one of his sons—a fine specimen known as Stephen—was filmed by MGM as a replacement trade mark but the film was never used. Stephen sired Finn II, born in 1947, who was the last of the original foundation stock.

During the period between the turn of the century and World War II we bred the lions and other cats in cages, which can cause problems. The most difficult thing is finding out whether the animals are compatible, before you introduce them to one another.

If you put two animals together which are not compatible, they will almost certainly fight, and possibly one of them will be killed. Most people may not realize this, but it's not simply a question of putting a male and a female together and letting nature take its course. We have tried mildly sedating them before bringing them together—to slow their reactions down a bit—but this doesn't always work. We tried it on a tiger and a difficult tigress and it merely had the effect of making them ignore each other completely.

When you put two animals of unknown temperament together in a cage, for mating purposes, you must always have somebody standing by with a high-pressure fire hose, which is about the safest method of separating them should they begin to fight.

During mating the male tends to grasp the female by the neck, holding her in his mouth. Afterwards she jumps back and snarls at the male. If she has been roughly treated her response may be quite aggressive. The male runs off and the female will perhaps pounce a short distance after him and then give up. In the confined space of a cage the male has no retreat and a fight could break out—hence the hoses. Now that the lions are in a spacious enclosure the male can slink off to a corner and leave his mate in peace.

Our second breeding line ended with two very well-known animals: a male, Cormac, born in 1959 and a lioness, Maire, born in 1961. Maire produced sixteen litters, five sired by her father Rusty, producing twenty-three cubs. Between 1966 and 1974, she gave birth to a further fifty-two cubs in eleven litters, all sired by her brother Cormac, beating Old Girl's record by a very comfortable margin. In all, she produced seventy-five cubs within twelve years. She is also the only lioness in captivity to have produced seven cubs in one litter; the normal litter is three or four.

One reason for her unusually large number of litters is that she was inclined to neglect her cubs, so we often took them away from her immediately after birth and hand-reared them. When cubs are taken from a lioness, because she is not feeding her young, she usually comes into season again within ten days. And since the gestation period is 106 days, it is possible to produce three litters from one lioness within one year. By the early seventies we had a small maternity hospital built for hand-rearing animals and we are now leaving it to my supervisor, Martin Reid, or to the keeper, Patrick Whelan.

These days I limit the zoo's lion population to one small pride—a male, two lionesses and whatever cubs happen to be around. They have an open air enclosure, where they can remain out of doors all the year round, and a warm shelter for cold nights. For a time safari parks, like those at Longleat and Woburn Abbey in England, served as a market for our surplus lions but they are now all stocked to capacity. The days of great demand for lions are over, so we breed only enough to keep our pride stocked and to meet the small demand from elsewhere.

When we decided to stop breeding lions on a big scale and go in for a wider selection of cats, concentrating as far as possible on endangered species, I received a letter from a friend of mine, who was travelling in South America, mentioning that he could obtain some ocelots for the zoo. They are beautiful, leopard-like creatures— just the sort of thing we were looking for.

I contacted him straight away and discovered that there were in fact a pair of ocelots available plus a kinka-jou—a South American bear, and a young tapir—a fascinating animal with the body of a pig, the neck and head of a horse, and an extended upper nose which looks like a trunk. I was thrilled at the prospect of these new acquisitions and set about obtaining the necessary import papers.

On the other side of the world, a thousand miles up the river Amazon, my friend, Gerry Kirkham, began to organize the transportation from his end.

Gerry was a seasoned traveller and was fascinated by wild creatures, particularly birds. He was throughly enjoying himself on his way back down the Amazon accompanied by his small menagerie—he discovered a macaw was also part of the deal—but his romantic ad-venture began to hit trouble when he discovered that it would take two weeks or more to get the export permits for the animals. He simply did not have that time to spend in Brazil.

He had, however, a friend, Jack Morris, who was in the oil business and who knew his way around Brazil: he suggested contacting one Jake the Rake.

Jake the Rake was a local beach-comber and smuggler. For the right price he could arrange anything. Gerry met him at a shady nightclub; it was no more than a thatched shack on the beach. Jake was not in the slighted bit daunted at the prospect of getting three ocelots, a tapir, a macaw and a kinkajou on to the boat on which Gerry was planning to sail for Ireland.

"Just give me the money," he said "and leave the animals with me. Ask no questions, and they'll be on board before you leave."

Gerry handed over the agreed sum, they shook hands on the deal and the next day the animals were delivered to Jake the Rake. Jack Morris assured Gerry that all would be well. Two or three days later Gerry boarded the cargo ship on which he was to travel and waited. At the last moment, just as the vessel was about to weigh anchor, a disreputable-looking fishing boat drew alongside and crates containing the animals were hoisted aboard. The crew accepted the cargo as if it was the most natural thing in the world. Unfortunately Jake, presumably economizing on packing cases, had put the two ocelots together and they had a fight in which one was killed. During the voyage the other ocelot managed by some means to escape and was found hiding in a small box on the deck of the ship. Using the ship's crane, a large, bottomless crate was lifted and placed over the small box with the ocelot still inside and it travelled to Liverpool in the crate. The macaw chewed its way out of its box and was on the loose throughout the voyage but nobody minded and it became quite a pet with the crew. The kinkajou also escaped and disappeared among a tangle of ropes of all shapes and sizes in the hold.

Some time later I received a call from Gerry in Liverpool. He had arrived and the animals were ready for collection from the docks. I rang my friend Freddie Williams at Chester Zoo and asked him to lend me some travelling cages and to meet me with them in Liverpool the next day.

Freddie Williams was waiting for me in the customs shed when I arrived there—but there was no sign of Gerry!

To reach the ship, we had to cross two other cargo boats moored beside it. The first thing I encountered when I went on board was the tapir, casually wandering around the deck. I picked him up in my arms and soon found that encumbered with this heavy creature, making my way back to the quay from ship to ship was no picnic. To the sailors and dockers watching, the whole thing was highly amusing.

However, I eventually made it and with Freddie's help loaded the tapir safely into one of the crates we had brought with us. The macaw presented no problems at all, nor did the kinkajou—once we had run him to earth in the hold.

Now only one problem remained: to get the ocelot ashore. They are quite savage creatures and this one was just about fully grown. The crew showed me the big crate with the smaller box inside it. We could see the hole in the side of the box so I asked Freddie to be prepared to cover it with a piece of wood we found close by. Then the crew lifted the crate away with a derrick, and as it rose up slowly, Freddie dived in with the wood and covered the hole in the ocelot's box. Holding the wood in place, Freddie and I then lifted the box together.

"Very light, isn't he," Freddie remarked.

"That's what I was thinking," I said, and at the same moment we both looked around. What neither Freddie nor I had realized was that the box had no bottom, and there was the ocelot, free and unencumbered, crouching on the deck, staring at us with his great, grey eyes. I think he was even more surprised than we were because he made no effort to escape or attack us.

Without a word and moving as one man—we had both been in this kind of situation before—Freddie and I turned around, still holding the bottomless box and slammed it down over the ocelot. Then we got a sheet of hardboard, slid it under the box, ocelot and all, and made our unsteady progress over the two intervening ships, up and down ladders and companion-ways to the shore. Here, after much careful manipulation we got him safely locked up in a crate for transport to Dublin.

It's really far easier to buy cats from a dealer or from another zoo. . . .

Public
Relations

I HAVE ALWAYS REGARDED running a zoo as a job which requires not only the ability to handle animals and enormous amounts of administration but also public relations skills, which I had luckily acquired, and the ability to deal with the most difficult animals of all—human beings. We are dependent upon our visitors for revenue and we therefore have to attract them to the zoo. Once inside it is our responsibility to provide an interesting day's entertainment and to cope with any problems they may encounter.

Attracting visitors involves a certain amount of show business—looking after and pleasing them once inside is always very simple—although there have been exceptions to that rule.

I made a positive effort to publicize the zoo as widely as possible from the moment I was promoted to assistant superintendent I used obvious methods such as newspaper advertising and attractive display posters, but I also jumped at any opportunity to get the zoo mentioned in any of the media.

One of my first excursions into the media on behalf of the zoo was a series of regular radio broadcasts. I was extremely nervous as I prepared for the first one and decided to take along an established and popular figure from the zoo to help me out. The whole thing was nearly a disaster and my companion was no help at all.

The cockatoo "Any Water" was world famous—a legendary bird who I remembered from my visits to the zoo as a child. She died in 1950 at the reported age of 104 years—70 of which she spent in the zoo yelling "Any Water" to successive generations of visitors. She said little else but never stopped saying that.

"Any Water" once landed a part in a play which required a tame, well-behaved cockatoo to appear on stage. Her part involved her sitting on the shoulder of the co-star, an actress called Nancy Price, at various times throughout the play. One evening the cockatoo completely stole the show. During a scene when Nancy Price, who was playing an old lady, was supposed to be dying, another member of the cast poured her a brandy from an elegant decanter. As the brandy filled the glass the cockatoo called out in a loud shrill—"Any Water, Any Water." A serious, dramatic climax was ruined as the audience roared with laughter.

Of course when I got the bird into the radio studio and announced over the microphone that she was with me, "Any Water" would utter not a syllable! Since an important section of my broadcast was devoted to the brilliant utterances of this cockatoo I had to improvise. The audience weren't disappointed; they heard "Any Water" coming through loud and clear, though the voice was Terry Murphy's heavily disguised.

When the Irish Television station opened I was invited to do a weekly programme about the zoo. It went well and other series followed, "Animal Trail" and

"Zoofari." They all opened with a long film sequence taken on location in the zoo, with yours truly doing the voice over. They ended with a studio interview during which I would introduce one of the smaller and more manageable animals to the public. The interview was televised "live" which always created problems.

For one programme, I brought along the kinkajou that I'd got from Gerry Kirkham. It was in a box with a lid over it, and I told the television crew to keep it out of sight and bring the box over to me at a certain point in the programme. I didn't want to hold the animal in my arms for too long as I thought the lights and the frenetic studio atmosphere might upset him. Kinkajous—which are also known as honey bears because they go after bees' nests in the wild and eat the honey—are tame enough and fairly easy to handle but it's asking a lot of any animal to remain calm in the bedlam of a television studio. It's not something I can do myself; I am never relaxed until the programme is safely over.

As I remember, I was telling the viewers about the kinkajou and what tame and gentle creatures they are when the crew slid the box over. I put my hand down, took off the lid and tried to lift the animal out to exhibit him before the cameras. As I did so, he gave me a very severe bite, closing his teeth on me slowly but relentlessly, like a pair of pliers.

I could feel this agonizing pain in my right hand, but I had to keep smiling into the cameras and chatting away while I transferred him hastily to the other hand. Needless to say the camera crew were laughing their heads off at my discomfort and madly signalling to me to keep my bleeding hand out of vision.

Getting the animals to the studio was another problem. Normally, unless it was an animal likely to cause trouble, I travelled alone and put whatever animal

I was going to show in a cage and placed it on the back seat of my car for the drive across town to Montrose studios, which are on the opposite side of the city.

One evening I was driving through the city centre with two macaws in a wicker basket on the back seat. The traffic was particularly heavy. Not only was it rush hour, but it was also Horse Show week, and on top of that I was rather pressed for time and getting a little panicky.

Suddenly I was aware of a great fluttering of wings behind my head. The macaws had amused themselves during the long delays in the traffic jams by biting their way through the wicker basket and were now causing havoc in the back of the car. I was in the middle traffic lane, so there was no question of pulling over to the side of the road and trying to get them under control; in any case, there was no time to stop. They started perching on my shoulder and biting affectionately at my ears and collar; it was a nightmare. I got some mighty peculiar looks from policemen on point duty, but I arrived safely in the end, and made it to the studio just in time. The programme went off without a hitch, the macaws were as good as gold. But I needed a stiff drink when it was all over. Before the programme started I had asked the studio people to ring the zoo and get Martin to come over with a fresh cage. I gave him the privilege of escorting them back to Phoenix Park; I'd had quite enough of them for one day.

So much for public relations outside the zoo—a relatively easy task. Inside the zoo it is also usually very straightforward. However, some people, seeing the animals looking calm and happy, do not fully appreciate that they are wild animals and not to be tampered with.

One one occasion a gentleman visitor actually climbed into an enclosure to retrieve his hat which had been blown in there by a gust of wind. The animals whose territory he invaded were the fallow deer—an entire herd of which run free in the Phoenix Park. Understandably he was not afraid to enter the enclosure but once inside he realized the folly of his ways. He was confronted by a large stag which proceeded to chase our visitor up a tree. Several keepers were called to the scene to rescue the poor man—and collect his hat!

A few visitors find things to complain about in the zoo—nowadays it is not so much the way we restrict our animals but the way the animals themselves behave. Not long ago I was standing close to two ladies who were watching a pair of chimpanzees mating.

"Isn't it disgraceful," one was saying, "that the people who run this place allow those animals to behave like that during opening hours when visitors, and that includes young children, are about."

"Oh, I don't know," the other replied. "They *are* wild animals, after all. Sure they don't know any better."

Apart from visitors feeding the animals, which is not as bad a problem as it once was, some also wish to bring their own pets into the gardens despite the notices prohibiting this. People simply do not realise that this practice is potentially dangerous.

On one occasion a woman managed to smuggle in a very small dog past the gatekeepers, and what's more, took it into the cat house. As it happened, I had a pair of leopards in a cage together hoping that they would mate. They became so excited at the sight of the dog that they clashed with one another in the scramble to reach the corner of the cage nearest to where the lady was standing, and within a few seconds the male had killed the female in the ensuing fight. It was all over before the keeper could reach the cage.

The explanation, of course, is that they both saw the dog in terms of a prey animal. It would have been exactly the same if I had walked up to the cage proferring a lump of meat. We never allow large cats such as leopards or cheetah to feed together in cages, it's far too risky. We separate them at night before they are fed. The lions, on the other hand, who live naturally in prides, eat together.

In general, the animals in the zoo are not easily upset. We're lucky in Ireland that the children who come to the zoo are on the whole very well behaved and rarely torment the animals as they have been known to do in other countries. You might come across one teasing a monkey occasionally but we never had any vicious behaviour.

What really upsets some animals are sudden sounds, like the backfiring of a car or the bang of the scare gun, and they find helicopters particularly disturbing. But they pay no attention at all to airplanes. Helicopters of course, fly much lower and make a dreadful racket. The clatter made by a low-flying helicopter is exactly the sort of disturbance that can make an otherwise docile and contented animal try to escape from its enclosure.

Some people regard zoos as the local sanctuary for unwanted pets and do not smuggle them in but come to offer them as new animals for the zoo. I had one lady call on me with a Mona monkey which she wanted me to take as it had grown vicious. I agreed to have it, if only because it might otherwise have been destroyed. We were moving it from her box to one of ours when it managed to escape and darted out of my office. It ran straight down to the lake, dived in and struck out for the far shore.

Most animals can swim if under stress, especially monkeys, many species of which are strong, natural swimmers. But for some species of monkey it is impossible because of their build. Spider monkeys and gibbons, for example, have such long, thin arms that they are unable to swim even small distances.

This lady had obviously heard that no monkeys can swim and as her pet leapt into the lake she became hysterical.

"It will drown!" She yelled. "Oh dear, the poor baby. Do something!"

"It will be all right," I said, trying to calm her down. "Almost any animal can swim if it needs to and that monkey of yours certainly can."

I sent for a boat to rescue the animal amidst a torrent of abuse from the lady.

"Monkeys can't swim," she yelled. "Anyone knows that. You'd let him drown."

"I have sent for a boat . . ."

"You shouldn't be allowed to be in charge of animals. You obviously know nothing about them. It's quite apparent that you haven't the slightest idea of how to deal with monkeys!"

"I assure you the monkey will be fine."

"No thanks to you. If I had not pointed out that it couldn't swim, you'd have let it drown."

"But they *can* swim . . ."

I was cut short as she slammed my door and headed for the lake herself, to watch her monkey come ashore with a keeper in the boat. It had managed to reach the opposite bank and was so exhausted by that time that it had made no attempt to resist recapture. As soon as we had dried the Mona monkey and allowed it to rest for a while in a cage in the heated interior of the monkey house, she insisted on taking it back home.

"It's quite obvious that you haven't the slightest idea how to deal with monkeys," she repeated to me indignantly. "I'm certainly not going to leave Tina with you." And they left.

This was a great mistake because although monkeys of many species make pleasant little pets when they are young, they almost invariably grow vicious as they get older and if they go for your face they can do a lot of damage. Also, various diseases are transmitted by monkeys some of which can be fatal to humans. For that reason I have always been resolutely against people keeping monkeys as pets and whenever I am asked to advise on which species makes the best house pet I reply: "None of them."

While I can understand people who take monkeys into their homes as pets, I cannot for the life of me comprehend why anybody would wish to make a pet of a reptile —yet many people do. In the Dublin Zoo, we receive regular telephone calls from people telling us that they've found a snake in their house or garden or office, and asking us to send someone along to deal with it. Most of these turn out to be quite harmless grass snakes which have been kept as pets and which have either escaped or have been deliberately released by their owners once they had lost interest in them.

I suppose the initial appeal is the novelty of the exotic but that soon wears off and they become a boring nuisance; I am, broadly speaking, against any interference with the liberty of the individual but I do think there is a case to be made for the prohibition of the sale of tortoises and indeed all reptiles by pet shops, especially to children who soon grow tired of them.

Not all the snakes we were called out to investigate were ex-pets of course, and not all of them turned out to be harmless. Quite early in my career, during Cedric Flood's time, we had a call from some terrified office girls in Brunswick Street, in the centre of Dublin, who said that a snake had dropped down from the attic into their office.

By the time I arrived on the scene I found that somebody had picked it up and thrown it out of the window into the yard below. At this stage I didn't know enough about snakes to tell by the look of it whether it was dangerous or not, but I had learned one thing: unlike mammals, reptiles have no means of maintaining their body temperature by converting the food they eat into heat; they have to rely entirely on the outside temperature to keep them warm, which is why they are never found in very cold latitudes. As soon as the temperature begins to fall, snakes become progressively more lethargic, until they appear to be anaesthetized.

So, although I didn't know whether this snake was dangerous or not, I could assume that because it was a very cold day and the poor creature had been lying in the yard for at least half an hour, it would hardly be very energetic. But to be on the safe side, I lowered a box, upside down, on a rope from the window and covered the snake with this before going down into the yard to investigate. When I very gently lifted the box to grab the snake behind the head, I found that it was almost unconscious with the cold, so I was able to put it in a small bag I had brought from the zoo and take it away without any trouble.

It was just as well that it was almost unconscious because it turned out to be a highly poisonous tree snake from South America. It had probably come into the country along with a bunch of bananas but how it got from the docks or from the greengrocer's into a Brunswick office is a mystery that we never solved.

One of the jobs I undertook when I first joined the

zoo, was assisting the keeper of the reptile house with
the snakes. They were fed, cleaned out and generally
"serviced" in the evenings after the public had gone.
During the winter months this meant working in the
reptile house after dark. The only light in there was from
an oil lamp and the weak glimmer it produced was quite
inadequate for this work. As we kept a number of
poisonous snakes in those days and as all the showcases
(you couldn't very well call them cages) were front
opening, this was a dangerous and unpleasant operation, particularly as snakes are far more active at night.
However, I gained a great deal of confidence from
the reptile keeper, Tommy Kelly, who had no fear of
snakes whatsoever and would grab the most poisonous
specimens without the slightest compunction. The trick
here, of course, is to grab them right behind the head;
held in this way, they cannot possibly harm you.

I have now become completely accustomed to
handling snakes. Most people have a horror of them but
they're not at all the cold, slimy creatures they appear to
be; in fact when you pick them up from their showcases, they are dry, warm and pleasant to touch—not in
the least repulsive.

I often went to London to collect specimens of
snakes, either as replacements for those we had lost
through natural causes, or to enlarge our collection by
including species not already represented. We brought
most of our snakes from Jack Lester in London Zoo. Kay
often came across with me for the trip, though she was
terrified of snakes and always hated the journey back. I
carried the snakes in a flour bag made of light canvas
through which they could breathe, and in order to keep
the snakes warm, I tied the bags around my waist, under
my jacket and overcoat.

In the early days we always travelled by boat and I

remember one occasion when I had placed the bag of snakes safely in a corner of the cabin where the heat was more than adequate, and had gone to bed, I was suddenly awakened by Kay.

"Wake up, Terry. Wake up!" She was saying. "One of those snakes has escaped. I can hear it hissing."

There was definitely a hissing sound in the cabin, but on investigation it proved to be coming from the central heating system of the boat. The snakes were safe and sound, and fast asleep in their canvas bags.

Snakes, as a matter of interest, are sold by the foot and the price varies according to the rarity of the species; at the time I'm talking about we were paying anything between £1.50 and £3.00 a foot for the more common varieties.

The customs officials at Holyhead and Dun Laoghaire got quite used to me coming through the barrier with this great bulge under my coat. Initially they were curious and wanted to know what I had in there but as soon as I mentioned the word "snakes" they were quite content to leave it at that.

Throughout the years the customs people, airline officials, stewards and pilots, the local police and all our visitors have co-operated wonderfully with the zoo and very often they have had to act on trust, respecting our judgment and guidance. I hope I can say we deserved this and that none of us connected with the zoo has ever abused our position. But one character deserves mention because at times he did lead our visitors a merry dance. The keeper who some years ago looked after the sea-lions was a great practical joker. Knowing that the public loved watching the sea-lions being fed, he would occasionally get a bucket of fish and walk all around the zoo with it. Seeing the fish in the bucket, the people would assume that he was on his way to feed the sea-lions and would follow him. Playing the part of a latter-day Pied Piper of Hamelin, he used to wander in a leisurely way around the backs of all the animal houses down to the lake, around the sea-lion pond and back again by the most roundabout route, with an ever-growing retinue tailing after him. Finally he would disappear into his own quarters before going down to the pond and actually feeding the sea-lions.

I have often wondered since just who was being fooled the most—the public or me—because that keeper managed to take lengthy breaks while having a bit of fun with the visitors and hiding out to confuse them.

The day Congola the chimpanzee escaped—*opposite* he faces me before heading off past some enclosures and towards the main gate.

Two new members for our pride of lions.

A magnificent male lion.

A snarl for the photographer from a lioness.

A Siberian tiger.

opposite I proudly display the three Siberian tiger cubs who were born in the autumn of 1978.

above Tiny leopard cubs in their enclosure.

left A black panther cub plays in our garden.

A leopard reveals its gigantic canines for the camera.

This ocelot provided a moment of drama when it arrived in
Liverpool from Brazil.

above A proud puma with her four cubs.

left Another of our fine cats—a lynx.

opposite A serval in its outdoor enclosure.

The orang-utan enclosure
viewed from across the
lake. The island in front
has proved to be a
successful home for the
gibbons.

The endearing face of a
Californian sea-lion.

Gusto the gorilla and I congratulate the little girl who was our 500,000th visitor.

An armful of snakes.

GOLDEN—MANTLED GROUND SQUIRREL

A chestnut mantle and a single broad white stripe on each side distinguish the
species from the rest of the Ground Squirrels.

Found in the foothill country and on mountain slopes of the west from the
Canadian Rockies to California.

Feed on seeds, nuts and fruit, frequently climbing trees in search of food.

All squirrels have internal cheek pouches where they carry seeds
and nuts to store in holes in trees and in the ground for the
winter, when they hibernate.

BREEDING: Mate in the early Spring and 4/7 young
are born in May and June.

Order: Rodentia   FAMILY   Sciuridae   SPECIES   Citellus lateralis

Around the zoo: *opposite above* a young hippopotamus and its keeper; *opposite below* a squirrel showing he is definitely in the right place; *above* the zoo in winter; and *left* a baby camel says hello to some visitors under a mother's watchful eye.

A fallow deer receives a friendly hug from a wallaby.

All In
A Day's Work

To ILLUSTRATE THE SORT of day-to-day problems
that arise in a zoo director's life, I will give an
account of the events in one day. I would say an
average day but it is so hard to find one without extraordinary events interrupting the routine. It is fair to say
this is my routine—interruptions included.

It is early summer and for the past week the weather
has been exceptionally good. As a result the number of
people visiting the zoo has created new records—up to
14,000 a day. To look after them, *and* the animals, we
have a staff of about 130. I'll take it hour by hour . . .

6:00 A.M. I wake up naturally each day at this time or
earlier. I go to the window to greet another glorious
morning. A faint mist is blurring the outline of the Dublin mountains, which might indicate a heat haze later. I
can hear the peacocks and the geese, the parrots and the
gibbons, coming to life.

As I dress and shave, I turn over in my mind a few
of the more immediate problems that must be faced

today. The gorillas have broken the glass front of their cage for the third time and the new, stronger laminated glass should be arriving. As I ponder this I make a mental note to arrange a meeting with the architect in order to discuss the new Gorilla House. Yinka and Gori will soon outgrow their present home and I have various ideas for their new enclosure.

I remember that there's a press conference arranged for noon. A wildlife expert who has just published a book about lions is in Dublin to publicize it and his publishers thought it might be a good idea if they introduced him to the Dublin press in the setting of the zoo, nursing one of our lion cubs in his arms, for the benefit of the cameramen; well, no problems there.

One of the giraffes is due to give birth; I don't anticipate any problems because she's had a couple of calves already, but I'd better get down to her stall first thing to see if there have been any developments during the night.

I make myself a quick breakfast and then set off on my rounds—it's clearly a morning for going on foot; on a wet day I might take the car and get it over as quickly as possible. Today I know I shall regret having to leave the zoo proper and retreat to my office.

By 6:45 A.M. I am walking towards the giraffe enclosure. The mother is in fine fettle, though there's no sign of the baby yet. She's calm and friendly, so I stroke her nose and tell her to hurry up and get on with it. It can't be more than a couple of days now.

I wander down towards the lake past the chimpanzees' enclosure and Congola, as usual, casually lobs a couple of stones at me. I think he's more or less forgiven me by now, but it's become a sort of tradition between us. The rest of the troop are all, like Congola, looking in peak condition; lying on their backs, enjoying the sun.

The penguins are wandering around, but the sea-lions are still lying lazily in a row on their island—a mass of rich brown fur. Crossing the lake, I let myself into the lions' den at the rear of their enclosure and have a brief word with them; they won't be allowed out until their keeper arrives. I then go and pay my respects to the Siberian tigers; they come to the bars of the indoor cage in which they sleep, and I ruffle the fur behind their ears and let them lick my hand. The three cubs, recently born, are doing well and they romp up to me, pushing each other over in the rush. Walking back over to the other side of the lake again, I pause for a moment to take a look at the flamingoes. This year, for the first time, we've had ten eggs, but I've taken all but one away and we're concentrating on a single breeding pair who have hatched their young.

Everything seems to be fine and the female is sitting close to her baby on top of the nest.

A quick check to see that all is well with the wilde-beeste. They've just had a calf, a male, and I'm wondering how long it will be safe to leave him in the same enclosure with the father. With a female, there'd be no problem, but two males, even a father and son, are apt to fight in an enclosure. Wildebeest are not generally reckoned to be playful, but these know me very well and always enjoy a little game; they run up and down along the edge of the dike and I'm expected to run with them. So far, the male doesn't appear to be showing any hostility towards the youngster, but I decide to have him moved today all the same.

Into the Monkey House next, where some of them instantly go into their various routines to attract my attention—swinging out on ropes, bouncing off the cage front or hanging upside down. The capuchins are particularly lively—grimacing at me and jumping up and down. They seem quite glad to see me despite the fact that they are indoors and not out on their island. A few days ago they all managed to escape and we are having to think carefully now about moving them elsewhere.

As it's such a beautiful morning, I open up the doors and leave the monkeys free to go outside. Most of them immediately turn on their backs and, like the chimps, soak up the sun.

I go in and see how the two gorillas are faring in their temporary night quarters. Clearly they don't like them all that much, but it is Gori's own fault that they are there in the first place. He broke the plate glass in a burst of excessive exuberance. Yinka the female, always friendly, extends a horny hand through the bars for me to clasp for a few minutes. I have a little chat with the pair of them; they don't understand a word I say, naturally, but they know the sound of my voice and seem to find it reassuring.

I wander into the Cat House to see the leopards, the black panthers and jaguars. They jump down silently and stalk alongside the glass panels.

I have a short game with them and then move on to see the female White rhino. As usual she comes snuffling over and appears to recognize me. That's another problem to be dealt with soon. She's on loan from London Zoo and I'm going to have to make arrangements to have her transported back shortly, because I've just had word that two young White rhinos which I recently bought will soon be arriving. The London Zoo will send the two White rhinos over to me in a large case divided by a partition and then, when they arrive, I can remove the partition and use the same crate to accommodate this rhino on her return journey to London. It can all be done in one day. I make a mental note to order a mobile crane to lift the crate over the railings into the rhino enclosure when it arrives.

A quick glance at the camels and hippos; not much sign of life there yet. It's getting late so I quickly visit the kangaroos and wallabies and then head back to the house.

7:30 A.M. I listen to the news on the radio and open my personal mail; the official letters will have gone straight to the office on the ground floor and will be dealt with by my secretary. I go down there and begin to write some letters.

8:30 A.M. The zoo staff are arriving and we are having alterations made to several of the houses, the building contractor's men are here also. I wander out to see how they are getting on. The new ape house is a big undertaking and we are also having a new cheetah enclosure erected.

As I turn to go back to my office I see Martin walking towards me. We go in to discuss the problems of the moment. One of the night security men has reported that the boiler in the Reptile House is not working properly; we also chat about the various repairs to railings and gates that need doing and then we decide to go over and take a look at that boiler.

9:30 A.M. Back in the office, I pass some letters to my secretary for typing and she gives me the day's mail which requires attention. I'm pleased at first when I notice there's an offer of an Indian elephant from a dealer in England. The price is incredibly reasonable and this makes me slightly suspicious because I happen to know that there's a severe shortage of Indian elephants in the British Isles at the present time. I make a few discreet telephone inquiries among people in the know about these things, and discover that this animal is rather too unruly for a zoo.

I've been looking for an elephant because we lost one recently in tragic circumstances. It died suddenly after a well-intentioned but foolish visitor gave it some food which caused liver failure. Many foods can be highly dangerous even to an animal in peak condition. It was a great pity that this visitor had not paid heed to the notices asking people never to feed the animals.

I decided to telephone my friend Jimmy Chipperfield who is always helpful when I need an animal urgently. He offers to lend me an African elephant until I can find a suitable Indian elephant. While the African variety is not as attractive, I am delighted to have acquired an elephant at all and I gladly accept his offer. We discuss the transport arrangements so that the animal can be delivered right away. As I begin to organize things at my end, Martin rings through. I'm surprised to learn that one of the wildebeest, who looked so content when I saw them earlier, has managed to get down into the dike by the enclosure and is refusing to budge. I go over. We cannot approach the animal too closely— they are often savage creatures—but we know it can easily get back up alone as we have opened the gate. We decide to leave him and hope he returns of his own free will.

10:30 A.M. Back to the office to deal with what might be described as the logistics of the job. I regret terribly having to spend so much time in the office doing administrative work.

Running a zoo is like running a small town; it's a community in itself within another, bigger community, Dublin city. We have shops, restaurants, bookstalls, refreshment kiosks, and there are always maintenance men working on something or other—the plumbing, the central heating, the electricity, the fencing. It's also a social centre; the 6,000 members have a restaurant where they can come for business lunches.

Mrs. Farrar who runs our shops rings me to find out how our new tie design is coming along. Her present stock of the old design is running low and she needs to know if it is worth her while ordering more of them if the new ones will be ready soon. The new design with a lion motif to replace the original giraffe is being created especially for our anniversary next year.

The next phone call is long distance from Finland. A zoo there holds the stud book on snow leopards and they have been helping me to locate a male to breed with the female I have acquired. I'm very pleased to hear that they believe there is a suitable male to be spared from Cincinnati Zoo in the United States. I ask my secretary to remind me to telephone Cincinnati that afternoon.

I get back to my mail and read an enquiry from a local artist asking to exhibit his work in our next exhibition of paintings. These exhibitions which we run occasionally have proved to be highly successful. I very much like the idea of utilizing the zoo in the evenings. I write a note to the artist asking to see some of his work. I'm afraid I'm no expert on these matters but so far no one has complained at my choice. I glance at my watch and realize it's time to get into the Board Room for the press conference.

12:30 P.M. The author and the publisher's publicity people have already arrived and so have some of the pressmen. We spend a pleasant hour chatting over coffee and biscuits as we wait for the television people. Martin takes my car, drives over to the lions' enclosure and borrows the cubs from the lioness for half an hour or so, and the author poses with the cubs while the camera shutters click.

In the middle of the press conference I'm called out for a few minutes because one of the secretaries wants a word with me. Today's quota of visitors includes a party of fifty children from a country school. The teacher with them has asked if they can have a guided tour from one of the keepers. I check with Martin who assures me we cannot possibly take any of the keepers off their usual duties. I agree and go back to the press conference. By now the cubs have been returned to the lioness, but in the meantime the television crew has arrived late so Martin has to fetch the cubs back from the enclosure. However, they've had more than enough human company for one day and have become restless and are inclined to struggle and whimper, so the effort is largely wasted because I know they're not going to use a single foot of film with the cubs in that ugly mood.

1:30 P.M. I escort the wildlife expert and the publicity people over to the members' restaurant for lunch. I rarely eat here—mainly because I cannot spare the time —but guests offer an exception. We have a delightful lunch but I am late in getting back down to work in my office.

3:00 P.M. The girl on the switchboard comes through to tell me there's a lady on the line from County Wicklow claiming that she has just seen a penguin in Arklow and that it must have escaped from the zoo and what am I going to do about it?

I tell the girl that I'll take the call myself; it's always simpler because I'm going to have to talk to her in the end.

I listen to her patiently and then assure her that it

couldn't possibly have been a penguin; none of our penguins are missing and in any case, as penguins can't fly, it wouldn't be possible for them to travel from Dublin to Arklow unless someone took them there by car.

"Then it must be a wild penguin," she says. "Because I saw it with my own two eyes."

I assure her that there are no wild penguins in Ireland.

"I happen to be a regular visitor to the zoo," she replies haughtily. "Kindly don't try to tell me that it wasn't a penguin. I know one when I see one!"

"I am quite sure that you believe you saw a penguin," I say in as soothing a voice as I can muster. "But it couldn't have been, because penguins simply don't exist north of the equator, except in captivity. It was probably a puffin—they look very much like penguins."

"You are being extremely rude. When my husband arrives home I'll get him to telephone you and then maybe you'll believe that I'm telling the truth. He was with me when I saw the penguin." And with that, she slams down the phone.

I pick mine up again and dial America. The people at the Cincinnati Zoo are extremely pleasant and helpful. They do have a spare male snow leopard which they are willing to loan to a zoo for breeding but another enquiry has already been made. I am assured that they will contact me shortly.

3:30 P.M. During a short meeting with our graphic artist to discuss new posters to advertize the zoo we are interrupted to be told a child is missing in the grounds. Naturally the parents are very concerned—imagining their little girl has possibly managed to come into contact with a wild animal. I assure them this is not possible and we go off together to try and find her. Within a few

251

minutes we spot her with one of the keepers walking towards us, and I get back to the posters.

4:00 P.M. A meeting of one of the Council sub-committees at which I present a report on the future development of the zoo. We discuss which animals we hope to breed and acquire over the next five years. Careful planning is crucial so that we can keep the zoo well stocked, maintain a constantly changing variety of species and use the space we have to the full. We also discuss the new enclosures and future building projects such as the Gorilla House.

After the meeting I stroll down to the lakes to check on the birds, particularly our young flamingo and the other baby chicks. As I return I am pleased to see the wildebeest is back in his enclosure with the others.

5:30 P.M. My secretary puts her head round the door to say goodnight as I settle down to work on a report I am preparing for a forthcoming conference in Frankfurt.

6:30 P.M. I stroll over to see the giraffe whose baby is due. She still seems calm and happy and I leave her, knowing that the closed circuit television is now on in the night security man's room. Walking back it is impossible to ignore the appalling amount of litter that has accumulated during the day. Ice cream sticks, cigarette butts, sweet papers and sandwich wrappings are everywhere. It is an unpleasant contrast to the unspoilt beauty of the zoo in the early morning, but a problem we have to live with.

Back indoors, after a quick wash and change into my slippers and a comfortable jacket, I pour Kay and myself a drink and stand by the window to enjoy the fading sun and a magnificent view. The mountains stand out clear and crisp against the deep blue sky. A flock of geese wheel in over the trees as they make their approach to land. They waggle their broad wings before skidding across the dappled lake with their feet spread out.

I'm looking forward to a quiet evening—a good meal, a little television and then I'll probably read for an hour or so before I go to bed.

The phone rings. It's the night security man.

"Sorry to disturb you but I think the baby giraffe is on the way at last."

As I'm phoning Martin, who lives close by, I kick off my slippers to get into a pair of Wellington boots, and exchange my jacket for an old sports coat just in case we have to enter the stall.

As I enter the night security room, Martin is already there and his broad grin tells me all is well. We carry on to the giraffe enclosure and creep inside in time to catch a glimpse of the youngster struggling to its feet and nuzzling up to its mother. For over thirty-five years I have shared my life with wild animals but the surge of joy within me when I witness a newly-born creature is as strong today as ever.

Martin and I tiptoe away and wander slowly homewards.

PICTURE CREDITS

The photographs are reproduced by kind permission of the following. *Daily Express* (Manchester): 181; *Daily Mirror* (Dublin): 184 (above); Dublin Zoo: 49, 50–1, 53, 56 (both), 57 (both), 58, 59, 61 (both), 63, 64, 109, 110 (below), 113 (both), 114 (both), 117 (below), 118, 119, 120, 174 (above), 175 (below), 176, 177 (above), 178 (below), 179, 182 (above left), 183 (above), 184 (below), 185 (below), 186–7, 226, 227 (both), 229, 232, 233 (below), 234, 235, 237 (below), 238 (above), 239 (both); Duggie Duggan: 52, 110–111, 112 (below), 115, 117 (above), 178 (above), 183 (below), 185 (above), 230, 236, 238 (below); Independent Newspapers Ltd. (Dublin): 54, 112 (above), 121, 180 (above), 182 (above right and below), 190, 233 (above), 240 (above); Irish Press Ltd: 173, 189, 240 (below), 242; *Irish Times*: 55, 111 (below), 116, 124, 175 (above), 177 (below), 228, 231, 237 (above), 241 (both); Irish Tourist Board: 180 (below), 188; Lensmen: 62, 122, 123 (both), 174 (below); *RTV Guide*: 60 (both).